NEW VISION FOR AN OLD STORY

New Vision for an Old Story

Why the Bible Might Not Be
the Book You Think It Is

Anne Robertson

WILLIAM B. EERDMANS PUBLISHING COMPANY
GRAND RAPIDS, MICHIGAN

Wm. B. Eerdmans Publishing Co.
4035 Park East Court SE, Grand Rapids, Michigan 49546
www.eerdmans.com

27 26 25 24 23 22 21 20 19 18   1 2 3 4 5 6 7 8 9 10

ISBN 978-0-8028-7457-3

Library of Congress Cataloging-in-Publication Data

Names: Robertson, Anne, 1959- author.
Title: New vision for an old story : why the Bible might not be the book
    you think it is / Anne Robertson.
Description: Grand Rapids : Eerdmans Publishing Co., 2018.
Identifiers: LCCN 2018015223 | ISBN 9780802874573 (pbk. : alk. paper)
Subjects: LCSH: Bible—Criticism, interpretation, etc.
Classification: LCC BS511.3 .R63 2018 | DDC 220.6—dc23
    LC record available at https://lccn.loc.gov/2018015223

To my father

You did not just read me stories;
You walked with me into other worlds
And, together, we believed.

Robert F. Robertson
April 18, 1933 – November 1, 1980

Contents

CONTENTS

Foreword

Praised be the Bible—big (too long), richly varied (poorly edited), audacious (every sacred cow and pompous person fair game), and odd. Most of us have a love/hate relationship with the sheer oddness of the biblical text, the distance that Scripture asserts even as it claims to bring God near. As literary critic Erich Auerbach said, "Scripture is more difficult than it ought to be."

The Bible is a human product that bears lots of the flaws and foibles that human beings bring to any of our creations. And yet the Bible is more. I'm convinced that there's no way that we could have come up with Scripture on our own. It's a foundational Christian claim that God insinuates into Scripture as nowhere else. Through the human words of Scripture, God breathes God's word to us, revealing, enlivening, encouraging, judging, reaching out to us to embrace us, while all we thought we were doing was reading an ancient book.

As a preacher, I've given thousands of sermons on as many biblical passages, but the lid will be screwed down on me before I do justice to the luxurious thickness of the Bible. I've been at biblical interpretation for nearly five decades, and I'm grateful that Jesus still uses this ancient book to shock and to baffle. We wouldn't have dared think up, on our own, a God who talks like the Trinity.

Even though I read Scripture every day, vast portions are still *terra incognita*. Only a fool would wander alone in Daniel or Lamentations without the reassuring protection of a first-class biblical commentary urbanely to explain that, while God may have said some strange things to some Jews back then, there's no way that God would say stuff like that to a thoughtful, educated person today.

When, as a seminarian, I complained about the difficulty of Paul Minear's course on the Gospel of John, a fellow seminarian advised, "Drop some acid. You'll find John makes more sense."

For those who enjoy pondering deep questions, for people who like thinking deep thoughts, the Bible is the book for you. And for anybody struggling to stay Christian, Scripture is a continually renewable resource.

I hope that my preacherly ruminations on Scripture help explain why I'm so excited about Anne Robertson's

New Vision for an Old Story. Anne is fully aware of the Bible's difficulty in gaining a hearing in today's world. And yet she passionately believes that the main impediments to engagement with the Bible are not in the Bible but in ourselves. Some of us who love Scripture have damaged the Bible's reputation with our uncharitable readings, our dogmatic assertions, and the false testimony we have given to Scripture. We have sometimes been guilty of forming the testimony of the Bible into our own image or to suit our own prejudices, and the Bible has thereby gained the enmity or apathy of many contemporary potential readers.

Anne has given much of her life to helping others fall in love with the Bible that she so unashamedly adores. In *New Vision for an Old Story* Anne argues that our chief problem with Scripture is the way we look at it. She offers a new "lens" for reading the Bible, a means of seeing and therefore listening to Scripture that highlights the Bible as story. Anne says that the Bible may not be the book you have been led to believe it is. Rather than law, abstract principles, or dogmatic assertions, the Bible is a long, wonderful, multifaceted story. Here is the story of God, who God is and what God is up to in the world. By implication, here is also our story, our history seen as an engaging narrative of the many ways God has stuck with us through the twists and turns of human history, a story with the happy ending of God with us, of God finally getting what God wanted from us all along—love of God and neighbor in Jesus Christ. Anne's hope is that you will read yourself into the story that is Scripture, and thereby you will find yourself looking at the world, yourself, and God in a whole new, life-giving way.

The other day a fellow professor, a biologist, said, "I have grown away from the church that I grew up in. But through the years, I've wanted to get back in the faith. I've felt a growing yearning to be closer to God. It's been a long time since I've done much Bible reading. Since the time I was in college, the Bible was always a problem for me to understand or to believe. I can't do it on my own. Have you got any books to suggest that might help me take another look at the Bible?"

Now I've got just the book to make the book called Bible come alive again, to speak God's word afresh, to give a new vision for an old story.

WILL WILLIMON

Introduction

What Do You See in the Bible?

There's no dearth of kindness in this world of ours; Only in our blindness we gather thorns for flowers.

—Grantland Rice

Back in 2012, Sears Optical made one of my favorite TV commercials. It begins with a woman stepping outside just before bedtime and calling for her cat. A raccoon waddles into view, and, mistaking the raccoon for her cat, she lets the raccoon into the house with the invitation "Come snuggle with Mama!" Then the ad cuts in to say "Missing something?" and proceeds to promote Sears's prescription eyewear.

With every year that passes, I'm more convinced there's a mix-up at the heart of most people's problems with the Bible, including the sometimes-violent conflicts that erupt over its application. Many of us get tripped up or fight about the Bible. But that's not because of what the Bible says, but because we don't understand what the Bible is in the first place. We come to Scripture expecting it to behave like a cat when what we're observing is a raccoon. As a result, we're missing essential understandings of Scripture along with the hope and joy those understandings can bring.

A few years ago I gave a talk in a Massachusetts church. One woman spoke to me afterwards, tears welling in her eyes. "Thank you," she said. "You've given me my Bible back." She never really thought about how she approached her Bible reading. She just read the words, found them offensive or naïve in too many places, and put the Bible in the pile of childish things she needed to give up.

What I said gave her a new way of looking at those troubling passages. She realized much of what she thought was a Bible problem was really a lens problem. She thought it was her cat behaving badly. But once she realized it was really a raccoon, everything made more sense. With that new vision, the woman was able to bring the Bible she loved as a child into her adult life without compromising her brain, her compassion, or her faith. The joy of that discovery brought her to tears.

My belief is that the Bible is God-breathed. You might have a different understanding, and we'll look at that general issue in Chapter 3. But, however you think of it, the Bible is a book with wise stories to tell and a profoundly hopeful view of the world. That wisdom and hope can speak even to those who choose not to subscribe to the religious faith this book represents. Too often we miss the Bible's value because our vision of its message is blurred and distorted by faulty lenses. After all, we're looking at the Bible from a distance of thousands of years. Every one of us needs glasses to see that far; the challenge is finding the right pair.

> *However you think of it, the Bible is a book with wise stories to tell and a profoundly hopeful view of the world. That wisdom and hope can speak even to those who choose not to subscribe to the religious faith this book represents.*

From the start, it's important to separate what we believe about the Bible *itself* from the question of which *interpretive lens* should be used to approach and read it. This is difficult, in part because when we read the Bible, we're often like that woman I met at church. We don't usually realize the assumptions we're bringing to our reading. We're just reading the words on the page, right?

Not really. Just say the word "Bible" to a group of people. Out drops an entire set of assumptions—as many as there are people who hear that word. Which assumptions those are depend on the person, but they usually have one thing in common: They're typically unconscious expectations that have never been critically examined. We have no idea they're there. We think we're reading with the naked eye, but we're actually reading through a thick, interpretive lens that may or may not be accurate. To bring those assumptions front and center, we need to change the question from "What does the Bible say?" to "What kind of book is the Bible?"

In 2016 the Massachusetts Bible Society, which I lead, conducted "The Great Bible Experiment: Exploring the Bible in America's Least Bible-Minded Cities" (massbible .org/experiment). To prepare for that series of events, we went out to Boston's Copley Square to ask random people what word came to mind when they heard the word "Bible." We had the poster about the project posted nearby.

The first thing we learned was that if you put up a big poster with an image of the Bible on it in the middle of Boston, No One Will Come Near You. People gave our crew a wide berth, and we got nowhere until we took the poster down. Once we did, the video cameras attracted attention, and people came close enough for us to ask our question: "What word comes to mind when you hear the word 'Bible'?" We still met with a problem. As soon as people heard the question, they scurried away without giving an answer.

Then we changed the initial question to this: "Would you like to be in a video?" People were intrigued and wanted to know what we were doing. "It's about words," we said. If we still had them then, almost in a whisper we could add, "It's about the Bible."

We still lost quite a few at that stage, but from those who were willing to respond to "What word comes to mind when you hear the word 'Bible'?," we had a range of responses. Many were what you might expect: "Truth," "love," "wisdom." But there were also words like "challenging," "scary," and "myth." Some who left without giving a response said only, "You can't print what I think."

When I crowdsourced the same question on social media, I was given a similar range of words—from "hope" and "faith" to "lies," "bigotry," and even "poison." That matched our Boston experience. Seeking support for a Bible society in Massachusetts is sometimes akin to trying to convince people of the medicinal value of arsenic.

That visit to Copley Square helped us to shape four town-hall-style events in four northeastern cities where a panel consisting of myself, a humanist, and a Catholic priest responded to audience questions about the Bible. What became clear in those events was that almost every question was rooted in one or more subconscious assumptions about the nature of and approach to the Bible itself.

For many, the Bible had been turned into a set of propositions and proof texts, and readers had no idea what they were missing. Our "experiment," as evidenced in our survey results, showed us that a new set of interpretive lenses made almost half of the 300 people who attended more willing to read and engage the Bible.

There are two basic approaches to the Bible that have saturated American culture. The first is viewing the Bible as a legal document—a book of rules and laws that demand our obedience. When we look through that lens, God is seen as judge and lawgiver; the rules are there in the Bible, and if you want to avoid punishment, you follow them. The second approach (often overlapping with the first) is seeing the Bible as a textbook. In this view, God is the author of all truth, and that truth is imparted literally and factually in the pages of the Bible. To question the literal meaning of the words on the page (which some groups expand to mean the words in their original languages on original documents that are as yet undiscovered) is to deny God and kick the Bible to the curb as "untrue."

There are two basic approaches to the Bible that have saturated American culture. The first is viewing the Bible as a legal document. The second approach (often overlapping with the first) is seeing the Bible as a textbook.

Those two reading lenses (or bifocals, if you join them) have had media amplification for a long time, especially in the United States. As a result, they're the default assumptions for almost everyone—conservative, liberal, atheist. People who have never even opened a Bible or set foot inside a church usually assume that either a legal or a literal reading are the only options. When I field social media attacks from Bible-haters who say things like "The Bible is just a bunch of myths and lies!," these people are assuming the textbook-style approach to the Bible as a primary source of facts. The accusation of "myth," in particular, assumes that factual truth is the only kind of truth there is. Actually, the scope of truth is much larger than merely things that are factual, which is something any real student of myth can tell you.

Likewise, when I'm speaking in churches of all denominations, I discover that Christians—like the woman I mentioned earlier—can have such a hard time with the Bible that they abandon it entirely. The most amazing thing is this: These same assumptions about the nature of Scripture lie unexamined across the theological and educational spectrum. When someone says the word "Bible," the weight of the symbol and the assumptions it conjures can crush your three doctorates with a single chapter.

When we start discussing those issues, as we did at "The Great Bible Experiment," we find that the Christian rejection of the Bible is frequently based in the subconscious belief that the Bible has to be read either as a book of universal rules that cannot be questioned or as a textbook of factual material that must be believed no matter what contrary evidence pops up in the physical or social sciences.

The Christian Right tosses the science and fearfully adheres to the rules as literally perceived. The Christian Left keeps the science, condemns the rules, and turns its Bibles into doorstops. Both wear either the scientific or the legal glasses—with predictably different responses and assumptions. In the following chapters we'll look at dismantling those assumptions in order to hold the pieces to the light of day. What emerges is not the need for a different Bible, but rather the need for a different lens.

The different lens we'll explore is story. Viewing the Bible through the lens of story can resolve many people's problems with Scripture and open its truth to those suspicious of its faith foundations—all without negating the hopeful and God-breathed vision I believe the Bible contains. A tall order, but that's why you have a book here and not a sermon. We'll be fleshing all of that out in the chapters ahead.

That said, switching lenses isn't an easy mission. Anyone adjusting to new prescription glasses can tell you that. Shifting an unconscious bias toward a new kind of reading takes practice and attention. It's like having a counselor point out that your knee-jerk reaction to your boss is really a reaction to having had an overly critical parent as a child. Even once you realize that's what's going on, it's still easy to slide into the old pattern. But we'll do this together, swapping lenses, chapter by chapter, and see how story opens the vista of a variety of biblical themes and issues.

You don't have to buy the lenses if you don't find them helpful. But—to return to the metaphor—if you're always screaming at your cat for destroying your kitchen, it may not be a cat you're dealing with. A new pair of glasses might help you see that you've let a raccoon into your home, that your cat is outside (and mad about it), and that when each is put in their preferred habitat, life is considerably calmer, and each is beautiful in their own way.

If you're missing something when you read the Bible, try on a new pair of lenses and see something new for yourself. You might get a bit dizzy as you get used to seeing in new ways. But soon you'll discover that there are things in the Bible that seem less problematic and more hopeful than they once did. Maybe you won't run the other way when people ask you for a minute of your time for your take on the Bible. Maybe you'll stay. Share. Talk. Yes, you can always go back to your old pair of lenses, but give the new ones a shot, just to *see*.

CHAPTER 1

The Story Frame

....

Invitation to Relationship

Stories have to be told or they die, and when they die, we can't remember who we are or why we're here.

Sue Monk Kidd
The Secret Life of Bees

"Let me tell you a story." It's the unspoken promise of every novel and film, of every painting, play, and ballad. It's the way that gifted teachers give instruction, and the way the best historians, poets, and sages convey their truth about the world. It's one of the few things that can coax a child into bed at night; and long, long ago, when families gathered around the fire to keep both wild beasts and chill nights at bay, it was the way that families, villages, and tribes learned who they were, what they believed, and who among them was brave or wise or pure.

The Bible is fundamentally a collection of stories—hundreds of them—arranged into "books" of larger stories which themselves then are bound together to form one grand story of hope, redemption, and restoration. Christian hymns are full of titles like "Tell Me the Story of Jesus," who himself taught his followers through the kind of stories we call parables. The entire Bible is story. Even the laws, genealogies, visions, and other kinds of details are told to flesh out a larger story of which they are just a part.

Not only is the entire Bible story, but the Christian mandate is to take "The Greatest Story Ever Told" and "Go, Tell It on the Mountain," or in some way to share the story, the Good News, the gospel that God has given us through the stories of the Bible. The way we share that story might be words, art, music, or the story of our lives lived out on the stage of the world. But it is all story, which means that, in order to properly understand the Bible, we need to know what stories are and what they're designed to do before we can learn to see the Bible through that lens or think about both the opportunities and the pitfalls of telling the story ourselves. That's what this first chapter is about.

The Stories that Bind Us

In all of life, stories are how we form, maintain, and define relationships. When we tell someone about our day, we don't just recite a list of events. We use the day's details as building blocks for a story about what our day was like and how we felt about it. That, in turn, gives us a bridge to nurture a relationship with someone else as we tell it and to find meaning for ourselves in what we do. Which is not to say that my Facebook post about last Thursday at work is going to win the Nobel Prize for literature. Sometimes it's a dull story; often it's a simple story; sometimes it's the same story day after day after day, and a loved one's hearing aid is discreetly switched to "off." But it's a story nonetheless, and it matters because, in the process of telling it, I'm inviting you into my life while trying to figure out my own small place and purpose in the world.

Stories not only help us communicate; they shape us. The formative power of stories explains why parents are usually very particular about which stories their children hear, read, and watch. As their impressions of life are first being formed, we want our children to share our worldview and to relate to others in the way we think is best, and we use stories to do it—stories that might be fictional but that we find to be "true" in deeper ways. We look for stories that are true to our values and that reinforce behaviors that we believe lead to success—however we might define that term.

When I was a child, my parents read me *Ferdinand the Bull* by Munro Leaf to be sure I understood that peace was better than fighting; and they read me *Winnie the Pooh* to teach me the joy of simple things, the importance of a good friend, and patience with the foibles of others. My father read me fantasy stories to be sure I knew that the world was a place of wonder and that what I saw with the naked eye might not be all there was to see. My parents took me to church so that I could hear the faith stories they valued and be introduced to the God they knew and loved. I went to school and heard the stories of our nation and learned what it meant to be an American. I learned what it meant to be from my particular school and from "Poor little Rhode Island, the smallest of the fifty states." Through books and television, through songs and news, through classrooms, church, and family tales told around the dining room table, I heard the stories that defined my relationship to myself, my family, my world, and my God. Which was exactly why those stories were told. That is what stories do.

As I grew and ventured out into the world, I learned that not every story was meant to be told everywhere. There were secret stories and dangerous stories and stories that you didn't tell unless you absolutely had to and maybe not even then. Not every story and therefore not every relationship was "safe." I learned the boundaries of my relationships through the responses I received to my stories and the effect that the stories of others had on me.

I also began to realize that there were other stories that belonged to other families, races, religions, and nations. To the extent that I could harmonize those stories with mine, my relationships and worldviews expanded. If I couldn't connect the dots, those stories, and therefore the people who shared them, were to me like some foreign land—to be engaged with curiosity or caution, maybe a bit of both, or maybe not at all. Stories don't just give you information or spin a tale. Stories weave a context of meaning that creates, defines, and nurtures relationships and all of our social bonds. Once those bonds are set, stories that give a different context of meaning can be difficult even to comprehend, let alone accept.

Some people object to teaching children Bible stories for that very reason—because they see the Bible as teaching a very narrow and exclusive view of the world that will make their kids lean toward bigotry and away from science. Others insist on teaching the Bible to make sure the laws and values found in the Bible are rock-solid as early in a child's life as possible. The debate plays out in school boards and educational circles from coast to coast. But underneath those arguments is the same basic misperception. Both fail to see the Bible itself as essentially story—to understand that the Bible doesn't just *contain* stories, it *is* story.

Human relationships at every level are forged by story, and the central invitation of the Bible is to discover a new frame for relationships with God, ourselves, and each other. Further, the God of both the Hebrew and the Christian Scriptures is described in personal, relational terms. The most natural way in the world for *that* God to shape and guide our relationships is through the oldest relationship-builder we know: stories. Viewing the Bible as story is totally consistent with the nature of the God who gave it to us.

The Dark Side

Stories are invitations to relationship within a given context of meaning, and our lives largely consist of choosing which of those relationships and contexts will shape and inform our lives. Our first stories are chosen for us by the circumstances of our birth. We are washed into this world in the waters of our racial, national, religious, and family identities and into the stories of what each of those means both separately and together.

As we grow, we begin to see how those stories affect the way we live and relate to others. We interact in an ever-widening circle of people, and we start to realize that there are other stories beyond our own. Would another set of stories and relationships help me cope a little better? We experiment. Sometimes we replace old stories with new ones. Sometimes we simply add stories to see if they help clarify the first ones. Sometimes we learn to see the original stories in new ways. Sometimes we realize a story we've grown up with has been the equivalent of being raised on pizza and chocolate-covered bacon. We thought it was great at the time, but it proves to be bad for us in the long run.

When a story we've heard and accepted rings true to our lives and we pass it along to others, it becomes the way we frame ourselves as friends, families, cities, and nations. Which is not to say that all stories are equally helpful. Sometimes a story that one group finds engaging ends up hurting another in ways both large and small, whether it's cliques in school, rival gangs, or warring nations. Dig into any conflict, and you'll find conflicting stories about each side's identity, experience, and view of the world. Stories have real, and sometimes deadly, power.

> *When a story we've heard and accepted rings true to our lives and we pass it along to others, it becomes the way we frame ourselves as friends, families, cities, and nations.*

Stories may be universal, but they're not neutral. Ever. Even the ones based in historical events. As Winston Churchill pointed out, "History is written by the victors." Just about every protest movement in history has been one group of people crying out that the stories being promoted by another group are crushing them. And just about every attempt at colonization has included an attempt to wipe out not just the stories of the other nation but the very language that gives those stories voice. Never let anyone tell you, "It's just a story." The stories we tell to ourselves and our children are powerful forces, as are the voices used to tell them. The words that so easily flow from our lips can bring justice or genocide, trust or tyranny. The wise frame their stories with care.

The Bible presents unique challenges in this regard because its length and complexity demand that we tell its stories in much smaller parts. To tell any story of the Bible requires removing it from its larger context, a task that is fraught with risk. When severed from the over-arching vision of healing and redemption, Scripture's darker stories or confusing passages can

> *To tell any story of the Bible requires removing it from its larger context, a task that is fraught with risk.*

be—and have been—misused for corrupt purposes. To hear the words "Bible story" and think the term is dismissive—that it's "just a story"—is to fundamentally misunderstand both the nature of stories and their enormous power. Later we'll look at the power of the storyteller more closely. Right now I want to stay focused on the nature of stories themselves and especially the particular set of stories we call the Bible.

The Family Bible

The story of the Bible is like the ancestral story of my family or yours. It has all sorts of characters; some we're proud of, and others we would rather not claim as relations. All kinds of things happen to those family characters in response to the waxing and waning of life across human history. Some of the family adventures you like to tell more than others. Some of them confuse you or make you angry, while others bring the comfort of a roaring fire on a winter's night. Much of it is contradictory, even to the values of the family whose story it is. But it's still your family and it's still somehow your story, even the parts before you were born and the parts that will come after you're gone.

That is the Bible. It's the family story of the people called Christians, who sprang out of the people called Jews, and it later helped birth the people called Muslims. You might read it as a family member, knowing somehow that the stories of the Bible are your stories, too. You might read it as one might read a biography of someone else, to understand a famous family that has left a notable impact on the world; or you might read it as someone who's married into a family whose customs you would like to know well enough to be welcome at a holiday dinner. You might even read it as one doing opposition research on a rival, looking for the skeletons in the family closet or holes in the defensive lines where you might gain an advantage.

But, however you encounter the Bible and for whatever reasons, if you don't first realize that it's a book of stories about the ways a particular people have seen and responded to the world across time, you will almost certainly misunderstand it. The Bible is not a claim that those people *should have* seen the world and responded the way they did. It is the story about how they in fact *did* see the world and how they *did* respond, warts and all.

Like every family tree, the Bible is filled with both saints and sinners—most typically, people who were some random mix of both. Most of them did the best they could with what they had.

> But, however you encounter the Bible and for whatever reasons, if you don't first realize that it's a book of stories about the ways a particular people have seen and responded to the world across time, you will almost certainly misunderstand it.

A few were simply scoundrels. Some made great choices and lived lives that made others call them blessed. Others not so much. That's what families are like, and that's what the family of the Bible is like. When 2 Timothy 3:16 makes the claim that all Scripture is useful for teaching righteousness, it doesn't mean that everything we read in the Bible is a model for how life should be lived. Sometimes we learn what righteousness is by watching its opposite and seeing the effect.

The means by which we learn those things is story, which always contains an invitation. The lens of story opens the door for us to read the Bible from the inside out. It's an invitation not just to read but to experience, to put ourselves in the shoes of every saint and sinner in the pages of Scripture and to learn firsthand what it means and how very hard it is to love God and your neighbor as yourself.

From the moment Adam and Eve eat that fruit and are cast out of the Garden, to the end of Revelation, when a new heaven and a new earth welcome people home, the entire Bible allows us to experience the vast, sweeping arc of people making mistakes, being sent off into exile, and ultimately returning to the metaphorical garden God had planned for them. Yes, there are laws, and genealogies, and way too many construction details for my taste, but those are always a smaller part of a larger story which is itself part of a still larger story, which reaches back to "In the beginning, God created the heavens and the earth" (Gen. 1:1) and forward to "The Spirit and the bride say, 'Come'" (Rev. 22:17).

The individual stories were recorded in a wide variety of places and times by a wide array of people. But that library of stories was selected, put into a certain order, and bound together as the Bible we know today so that the individual stories could be seen together as one expansive story—intentionally told in order to form those who hear it into a beloved community who will bear witness to the love of God in this world. I know, I know. It hasn't always worked that way. We'll talk about that. But sometimes it has, and when it hasn't, the culprit has frequently been a misunderstanding of the Bible. And when the Bible is misused by otherwise good people, it usually means they've been reading it with lenses made for something else.

That's why I'm writing, and that's why you're reading. So, let's move in closer to explore our eyewear options.

CHAPTER 2

The Optics of Truth

Seeing Through a Dark Glass

Perhaps the truth depends on a walk around the lake.

—Wallace Stevens

We are never detached from a good novel or film. We eagerly accept the story's invitation to enter that world, and we easily form relationships with its characters, shed tears over their losses, and dress up like our favorites for Halloween. We feel like we know them. I've read novels with characters so vivid that I've actually dreamt about them. If we can recognize that same invitation in the stories of the Bible, important new ways to engage it emerge.

And yet, many people are resistant to seeing the Bible as story, a reluctance frequently rooted in questions over what it means to say that the Bible is "true." People hear "story" and think "fiction," concluding that the word is dismissive of the truth of the text and, by extension, God. If you ask Christians what the difference is between the Bible and *Star Wars*, a large number of them would answer, "Well, the Bible is *true*." Pull up a chair.

Looking through the Options:
The Many Lenses of Truth

Debates about the "truth" of Scripture are endless and heated, and a good many of those arguments are a product of the lenses we use to find the Bible's truth. While it won't solve all our Bible problems, it's important at least to be aware that different lenses see and define truth differently. Think of it as the rear-view mirror on a car which frequently alerts us that "objects may be closer than they appear."

There are a variety of standards for what gets stamped with the label "true," often related to different academic disciplines and professions. In science, truth is largely equated with facts. Proof is established by some objective means, which other people then are able to replicate with the same results. A slightly different standard applies in law, where a combination of objective facts and human experience (i.e., testimony) are presented in a trial and given to a judge or jury to determine the truth. In journalism, you run with a "true" story when you have multiple sources who have been vetted for their reliability in the past. All those lenses rely on some form of consensus about observable behavior, with varying degrees and types of credentials expected in each instance.

When you move into the arts, the definition of "true" shifts dramatically and becomes much more subjective. A portrait might be considered true because it captures the exact details of a person's face; but it also might be a more abstract style that truly captures a person's personality through light, color, and shape. In literature, the word "true" is used in a variety of ways. Sometimes we talk about "true" stories to distinguish a biography or a historical novel from works of pure fiction. But we also use the word "true" when a work, fictional or otherwise, resonates with human experience. It is "true to life" or "true" to the experience of a given culture or common human situation. Consider these words from the children's book *The Velveteen Rabbit* by Margery Williams:

> "Real isn't how you are made," said the Skin Horse. "It's a thing that happens to you. When a child loves you for a long, long time, not just to play with, but REALLY loves you, then you become Real."

In reading this explanation, we recognize right away that it is "true." It's how love works, even though the story is a work of fiction. Science glasses would read *The Velveteen Rabbit* as absolute rubbish. Seen through those lenses, the story would easily be labeled "false." Of course a stuffed rabbit can't become real! But with the lens of story, the truth that catapulted the book to the bestseller list is easily visible.

In Victor Hugo's classic, *Les Misérables*, the tragedy of using a purely legal lens for the life of a man is one of the main points of the novel. The tragic figure of Inspector Javert has no way of understanding a story of poverty that might lead a man to steal a loaf of bread or a story of redemption that could turn a thief into a productive and praiseworthy citizen. Javert sees only laws that are kept and laws that are broken. It's such a flawed lens for the totality of life that Javert's legal focus turns his own humanity against him, and he takes his own life. Meanwhile, the escaped prisoner he chased to the ends of the earth is ushered into eternal bliss. Hugo's story tells us the lens of the law isn't sufficient for seeing the truth of life, love, and relationship. You need the story lens for that.

Some of the largest issues people have with the Bible (and, by extension, with the church) today have come about because many of the loudest voices in our culture look at the truth of the Bible as if it were a legal code or a textbook of facts. The lenses appropriate for those disciplines see truth very differently than the lens of literature does, and the result can be deep misunderstanding and misuse of the Bible. This is not to suggest that the Bible is just another book of great literature on a par with all the others, but rather that the literary understanding of "truth" is more suited to the meaning and depth of the Bible than the criteria of other disciplines.

> *The Bible is a collection of stories meant to invite us into a loving relationship with God and, by extension, with each other. If we see it as a legal code or a textbook, we can easily lose the thread of loving relationship it is meant to foster.*

The Bible is a collection of stories meant to invite us into a loving relationship with God and, by extension, with each other. If we see it as a legal code or a textbook, we can easily lose the thread of loving relationship it is meant to foster. The story lens won't eliminate every issue we have with Scripture, and we might still disagree with some or all of its message. But if we aren't looking at the Bible through the lens of story, we won't understand that message well enough to make a determination. We literally won't be able to see it.

The Bible as Law: The Ten Commandments

One of the best-known displays of this misunderstanding involves the Ten Commandments. We first encounter them as a gathered list at the start of Exodus 20 in the Hebrew Bible, but the lead-in really starts in the previous chapter. There God reminds the former Hebrew slaves of the story of their liberation from Egypt and offers, "If you obey my voice and keep my covenant, you shall be my treasured possession out of all the peoples." Hearing that offer and remembering the story, the people respond, "Everything that the LORD has spoken we will do." Offer made; offer accepted. And the people take three days to prepare for the formal commitment ceremony at the foot of a fiery mountain.

To Jewish ears, this is the story of a betrothal and a marriage, including a standard of ten behaviors that secure and guide the relationship. The Ten Commandments are like the typical wedding vows to love, cherish, and be faithful, not the household rules about who takes out the trash. It's not the imposition of a legal code, even though those behavioral standards would come to serve as the umbrella for all the actual laws of the new nation of Israel. Jews don't even call them the "Ten Commandments." They are simply the "Ten Words," a title taken from the very beginning of Exodus 20: "Then God spoke all *these words*."

For Jews, this is not primarily a legal text; it's a relational one. The covenant relationship sealed here is rooted in the story of their journey together as God and people. The First Word for Jews is the remembrance of that story: "I am the LORD your God, who brought you out of the land of Egypt, out of the house of slavery." If you see the text as Jews do—as a story about a covenant relationship—you would never dream of posting the Ten Words in public places and insisting that those who didn't even come to the wedding must obey them. Making them into law would be like pulling two people off the street and insisting that they marry each other. The story is about a voluntary covenant between a grateful people and the God who liberated them. It's not a shotgun marriage. That's what the story lens shows.

Christians often mistakenly focus on the legal lens and see this passage in Exodus as God laying down the law—which is why, in Christian circles, it's always called the "Ten Commandments." For Christians viewing this as a legal code, that verse about God bringing the Hebrews out of Egypt is just introductory material before getting to the main event—the commands about what we shall or shall not do.

It's telling that the cultural controversies swirling around the Ten Commandments are all rooted in viewing the text as a legal document instead of a relational one—as law instead of story. As a legal text, it becomes subject to a different test of "truth" than one based in the story of a relationship. If you see Exodus 20 as God laying down the law and literally carving that law into stone while the mountain around you is quaking with fire and smoke— well, you tend to give those laws more weight and assume they must be THE law for ALL time. It's Truth with a giant, fire-breathing T.

Once you're that far, it feels like a mandate to impose that law on everyone, to hang it up everywhere and demand obedience of every person. A story of liberation and grateful response thus is replaced with a legal basis for coercion. It's that legal view of Christians and not the relational view of Jews that causes the conflicts in courtrooms, schools, and town halls. And because those are public conflicts, they get public attention, which amplifies the mistaken message that the Bible is to be read as a legal text. Those outside of the faith entirely then come to view Christians as cruel, the faith as oppressive, and the Bible as the Christian weapon of choice. Those observers can cite many horrific examples to back up their claims.

But these terrible misapplications rarely happen when we use the literary lens of story. Those with a relationshipbased view of God's words at Sinai kick back with their beverage of choice and roll the story around on their tongues until the full taste has been absorbed. Since they don't view God's words as a legal document, they aren't focused on the fear of punishment, which gives them time to think and ponder, enjoy and question. With the story lens, there's time to think about how these events might relate to stories from elsewhere in the Bible, from another book entirely, or even from your visit with family last week. There is freedom to ask all kinds of questions. "What does having no other gods really mean in my world today?" "Murder ... hmmm ... does that include capital punishment?" "Wow—look at that Sabbath thing. This is a God who guaranteed everybody a day off? Even the slaves and cattle? Can I get some of that?"

Some of those questions may lead to debate, and many lead to still further questions and research; but a relational and covenantal view of the Bible invites rather than forces people into the text. It encourages seeking rather than mandating what someone must find. Later in this book we'll explore the different tolerance levels that people have for unanswered questions and how those affect people's willingness to engage the Bible. But for now it's worth noting that how we view the basic nature of the Bible affects how we read it and what "truth" we glean from it.

The Bible as Textbook: Jonah

Viewing the Bible as a textbook is similar to taking a legal view, since textbooks present a kind of rule or law. The implicit claim of a textbook is that the contents contain facts that can be objectively verified, and, if you want to engage the field that the textbook represents, those facts are the rules you will have to learn and follow. We call them the "laws" of science or the "rules" of grammar for a reason. If you don't learn the laws of chemistry, decidedly unpleasant things can happen in the lab.

In the world of textbooks, what is labeled "true" is only what can be objectively proven and replicated over and over. So, if you see the Bible as a compendium of facts constituting a textbook, you suddenly have to prove those facts in a way that everyone will accept and understand in only one way. Since abiding by the facts of a textbook is necessary for acceptance within a given discipline, those who ignore the facts are cast out of the circle. When applied to Christianity, a textbook-based approach ends in conflicts with science, heretic-hunting, and various claims regarding who may or may not be considered part of the faith.

The trouble is, you can't prove God exists in the same way you can prove that $2 + 2 = 4$. God can't be proven or disproven in a lab. The truth claims about God and religion are known in other ways, and the most basic of those is through the stories of the people who take those truths on faith and try to make a go of it in the world. There are thousands of years of those stories in the Bible, but let's pause and take a look at how a textbook approach can divert our attention from the real truth of a biblical story. Meet Jonah.

If you've never read the book of Jonah, consider giving it a go; it's only a few pages long. But here's the abbreviated version: God tells Jonah to go to the people of Nineveh and tell them to quit being so wicked or God will destroy their city. Jonah refuses and gets on a ship headed in the opposite direction. Why? Is he afraid of the task? No. He refuses to go because he hates the people of Nineveh, knows if they hear God's call they'll repent, and knows God will reward that repentance with blessing. He doesn't want God to bless them. He *wants* God to rain down fire and destroy them. So, he bolts.

God isn't pleased with this behavior and causes a storm at sea that threatens the ship on which Jonah is fleeing. The crew knows that God's upset about something, but they don't know what. They start throwing supplies overboard, trying to keep the ship afloat. Then Jonah fesses up. He explains to the crew that the storm is his fault and tells them to throw him overboard instead. Fearing for their lives, they do. After a giant fish comes and swallows Jonah whole, the storm abates.

Jonah lives in the belly of that fish for three days, and then the fish vomits him up on the shore. Unfortunately for Jonah, God hasn't gone anywhere and still has the same order: Go to Nineveh. In light of his recent experience, Jonah decides that this time he will follow directions; so he goes, telling the people of Nineveh to repent. When they do, their destruction is averted. Happy ending, right? Well, not for Jonah, because his hatred of the Ninevites wasn't really based on their actions. It was pure bigotry. He wanted God to destroy them, which is why he ran in the first place. Now Jonah responds to their repentance with a temper tantrum:

> "O LORD! Is not this what I said while I was still in my own country? That is why I fled to Tarshish at the beginning; for I knew that you are a gracious God and merciful, slow to anger, and abounding in steadfast love, and ready to relent from punishing. And now, O LORD, please take my life from me, for it is better for me to die than to live." (Jon. 4:2–3)

Jonah would rather die than watch God bless people he hates. That's a serious bigot, and you have to wonder if trying to pry open Jonah's hard heart wasn't one of the reasons God chose him for the task in the first place. Before the story of Jonah ends, God has one last little object lesson before making the point that ends the book: "And should I not be concerned about Nineveh, that great city, in which there are more than a hundred and twenty thousand persons who do not know their right hand from their left, and also many animals?" Mic drop.

This story is powerful on many levels, but if you go to a Bible study on Jonah, you'll notice that people get hung up on whether the story is factual. They've got their textbook glasses on. Did Jonah actually exist? Is there a species of giant fish that could swallow a man whole? Could a man survive three days in the belly of such a fish? In focusing on those questions, the "truth" of the story becomes totally bound to whether the story is factually sound. All of a sudden it has to pass the textbook test. The arguments start, the search engine rankings for "giant fish that can swallow a person whole" rise, and before long the Bible study is over, people are divided, and no one has come even close to the "truth" of the story of Jonah. Depending on the group, they may also get caught up in whether God can perform miracles. The fish may just as well have swallowed the group.

When you really understand the Bible as story, you begin to understand it doesn't have to be factual in order to be true. Looking at Jonah's tale through the lens of story takes off the table all the arguments about whether Jonah could have been swallowed alive by an actual species of fish. Maybe it happened or maybe it didn't. That's not the point. It was never the point. The story of Jonah was not fact-checked by ichthyologists. Nineveh happens to be an actual city, once the capital of Assyria, now pretty much a pile of rubble in Iraq, just across the river from Mosul. But it wouldn't have mattered if it was Seattle or some totally made-up city, because the story of Jonah isn't about facts. It's about the hard truths of obedience and bigotry and God taking a fish-vomiting torch to hardened hearts in order to teach us that God cares about people outside of our own tribe and country.

Looking to the Bible for the kind of truth we find in textbooks is the chief culprit behind the battles between religion and science and can devastate our ability to read Scripture. That approach also hurts the image of the Bible in the broader world in the same way that reading the Bible as law does. It drives people from church pews, and those outside of Christian faith come to view Christians as idiots who don't have even a basic understanding of how the world works.

> *Looking to the Bible for the kind of truth we find in textbooks is the chief culprit behind the battles between religion and science and can devastate our ability to read Scripture.*

The public nature of these battles again leads to media attention, which leads to amplifying the mistaken message that the Bible is supposed to be a textbook full of facts. Bible foes grab hold of that, and the next thing you know, those of us trying to defend the Bible are hit with accusations that we should get rid of it because it's just a bunch of "myths" and "lies," terms these foes base on the false assumption that the Bible claims to be a compendium of facts, while they miss the understanding that myths have transmitted truth for millennia. The giant fish swallows almost as many of the Bible's detractors as it does its supporters.

Religion has no more business wandering into a geology class and saying the earth is only six thousand years old than science has in walking into church and saying God didn't create the world. Science trades in facts, and religion trades in the much broader category of truth. There are helpful ways they can and should inform each other, but the way they each determine whether something is "true" is vastly different. They can and should be in conversation, but the two should not be confused or conflated.

Facts are critically important, and yes, we want actual facts in our textbooks. I don't want the FDA determining whether my food is safe by reading poems about wheat fields. I want hard, unmanipulated, scientific data. I don't want NASA basing their missions on *Goodnight, Moon*. The point is not that facts are irrelevant to our lives or that there are no facts in the Bible, but that the Bible is not intended to give us primarily factual truth. This means that looking at it with fact-seeking lenses will blur the truth it is trying to give us. The Bible is designed to give us relational truth—truth about how to live in loving community, how to understand and shine light into the dark corners of the human soul, how to love God and to love our neighbors as ourselves.

Seeing Truth Through a Dirty Glass

One of the most important truths that the Bible tells is actually straightforward. It comes from Paul's first letter to the Corinthians in the famous thirteenth chapter that is so often read at weddings and funerals: "For now we see in a mirror, dimly, but then we will see face to face" (1 Cor. 13:12). In the King James Version it says we see through a "glass, darkly." The message is the same: In this life, our vision of reality—of truth—is not clear, even if we're wearing the right lenses. It's a dim mirror, a dark glass, a dirty window. Limited vision is part of what it means to be human, and the proper response to that limitation is humility.

That limitation is exactly why stories are the fundamental building blocks of life and, by extension, the Bible. We can't describe the truth about God, the world, or even ourselves with direct clarity. We can only say "Call me Ishmael," or "It was the best of times, it was the worst of times," or "There once was a man who had two sons." We have to look from the side, through a prism, and try to distinguish between the dirt on the glass and the actual nature of the thing on the other side.

Some strains of philosophy claim that all truth is relative—that every person has their own truth and nothing is absolute. That doesn't strike me as a full picture. I do believe that there is absolute truth—that there is something definable on the other side of that glass. We just can't see it clearly or completely. Every person is looking through the same huge window at the same absolute truth, but every one of us is looking from a different angle with dirt and dust obscuring different things from our view.

Consider the old Indian fable called "The Blind Men and the Elephant." My favorite version of that is by the American poet John Godfrey Saxe (1816–1887):

> It was six men of Indostan
>> To learning much inclined,
> Who went to see the Elephant
>> (Though all of them were blind),
> That each by observation
>> Might satisfy his mind.

The poem goes on from there to show each of the six men holding on to a different part of the elephant and proclaiming that they alone know what an elephant is like from their personal observation. One touches the animal's side and declares the elephant is like a wall, another holds the tail and argues an elephant is like a rope, while the guy grasping the trunk says it's like a snake, and so forth. And what do they do with their various experiences of the elephant? As Saxe puts it,

> And so these men of Indostan
>> Disputed loud and long,
> Each in his own opinion
>> Exceeding stiff and strong,
> Though each was partly in the right,
>> And all were in the wrong!

Moral:

> So oft in theologic wars,
>> The disputants, I ween,
> Rail on in utter ignorance
>> Of what each other mean,
> And prate about an Elephant
>> Not one of them has seen!

One of the greatest linguistic tragedies is the disappearance of the word "prate" from common English usage. Oh, how we like to "prate on" about the God we have not seen, except in part through a dirty glass. I've been to those church meetings, and likely so have you. When different people have different experiences of God or of life more generally, we have a choice. We can "prate on" about how our view is the right one, or we can exercise curiosity and humility and listen. The stories that we will hear invite us into the lives of others so that we might better understand their different perspectives. The future of human community may well depend on our ability to prate less and listen more.

You Shall Know the Truth

"You shall know the truth, and the truth shall set you free," Jesus said. Given all we've discussed, what does it mean to say you "know" the truth? What is that different kind of knowing that applies to religious truth but not necessarily to objective facts? Conveyed through story, and seen through the lens of literature, "knowing" a religious truth is something we understand as relational—not just something one person figures out in a vacuum. It is experiential, not intellectual.

The truth of the Bible isn't about doctrine and dogma. Those are legal things that govern the way specific faith communities agree to conduct themselves. The Bible isn't primarily a legal book; it's a relational book—story, which means that in order to really "know" the truth, the things we accept on faith must be tested in the fires of real life.

Jesus said, "I am the way, and the truth, and the life" (John 14:6). For the Christian, truth is not a *what* that we understand with our minds, but a *Who* we can love in our hearts. It is found and known in loving relationship. While there are certainly facts that can be known about Jesus, to turn Jesus into a fact is to take the truth and therefore the deity right out of him. It is also to block the hope of relationship both with Jesus and with others in His name. The truth at the heart of the gospel is experiential; it is relational; it is story. Why would the Bible that proclaims that message be anything different?

> *The truth of the Bible isn't about doctrine and dogma. Those are legal things that govern the way specific faith communities agree to conduct themselves. The Bible isn't primarily a legal book; it's a relational book.*

CHAPTER 3

Squinting for God

Did God Inspire the Bible?

*A common mistake we make is that we look for God
in places where we ourselves wish to find him.*

—Criss Jami, Killosophy

The question of God's involvement in the creation of
the Bible matters a lot if you see the Bible as a legal
document or a science textbook, because truth in those
disciplines is dependent on the reliability of the source.
If the authority behind a law or the source of a fact is
discredited, the information they contain goes down
with the ship—as it should. You don't want a fake attor-
ney representing you in court, and you don't want your
surgeon following the instructions on a YouTube video.
But the Bible presents a different kind of truth than that
of law or science, which means that the debates about

its relationship to divine authority are also considered differently.

It's a Raccoon

A woman who attended my Bible study series in her church came up to me later at a conference. She told me that learning how the Bible was put together had shaken her. "It's rigged!" she said in dismay. "They all had agendas—it's rigged! I don't trust any of it." Such faith-shaking is as common as rain in the first year of seminary. Why? Because many seminary students come into their first classes as that woman did to the Bible study—assuming either a legal or a scientific lens for the truth of the Bible. And when you're wearing those lenses, you can't have human beings playing any significant role in shaping Scripture for the reasons I outlined above.

But when confronted with the very human history of the canon, individuals with those initial assumptions are blinded by the full light of day. At first, many, like the woman who spoke to me, feel lost. Their glasses fog over, and nothing seems clear anymore. They were led to believe that if fallible humans meddled with Scripture, then the truth of the Bible wouldn't be reliable. A host of dizzying questions then come pouring in. "Did humans mess up everything, or are there some passages I can still trust? And how do I know which ones they are?" "Does the translation matter? Which is the 'right' one?" And, most critically but less frequently spoken, "Is my salvation in jeopardy if I can't sort this out?"

The next thing you know, people are sparring over whether saying the Bible is "inerrant" or "infallible" means there are no errors or inconsistencies in a particular translation (cue debates over which translation gets it right), no errors in the original languages (which means you have to study the biblical languages to know the truth), no errors in the original manuscripts (not one of which has yet been discovered), or whether it is without error only in specifically religious matters (the Roman Catholic position). The competing claims, most of which declare you're hell-bound if you disagree, can make people want to just put the lid back on the Bible box and go study something less chaotic. Like quantum physics.

Often no one is there in such moments to catch people who feel like they're in freefall. On one side they see scholars, who frequently look on their struggles with more bemusement than compassion. On the other side they see the people who nurtured the faith that brought them to study the Bible in the first place, who now are telling them this new knowledge is heresy and calling on them to recant or be cast from their fellowship. Students feel pressed to make a choice: faith or scholarship, religion or science, loving community or intellectual integrity. Moving forward with both can make them feel like old Marley dragging around the heavy chains of his past, so most just pick one side and move on.

But here's the thing. There are no sides. That's a false choice. The words "inerrant" and "infallible" are only visible within a legal or a scientific framework. The crisis is unnecessary, and it disappears entirely if you're looking at the Bible through the lens of story. Recently someone on Twitter asked, "So are you saying the Bible is wrong?" There's no way to answer that question because the premise is skewed. Right or wrong, inerrant or faulty, are inappropriate categories for evaluating the Bible. It's not that kind of book.

> *But here's the thing. There are no sides. That's a false choice. The words "inerrant" and "infallible" are only visible within a legal or a scientific framework. The crisis is unnecessary, and it disappears entirely if you're looking at the Bible through the lens of story.*

Remember the illustration from the introduction of the woman with poor eyesight? Mistaking a raccoon for her cat, she let it into the house. The binary choices like those above exist only while you're wearing your law/science bifocals.

My glasses for distance are great for driving, but if I'm trying to read the instructions on a medicine bottle, I can't see a thing with those lenses. I have to put on my reading glasses. And neither of those lenses are helpful for the mid-range vision of working on my computer. In the same way, while we need the lenses of facts and laws for some subjects, we don't see clearly through them when looking at the Bible. It's not a cat; it's a raccoon, and our spiritual houses will be in chaos and conflict until we can clearly see what we're dealing with and put the raccoon back into its natural environment.

If the Bible is essentially story, it's the truth of literature and not of law or science that we expect to see. We see *stories* as true when they resonate with life as we know it. And that's exactly why learning about how those stories came to be is not a faith-shaking moment. When I read about how movie technicians turned Andy Serkis into Gollum in *Lord of the Rings*, that didn't shatter either the wonder of the films or the truths about the complexity of evil that his character presented. That truth springs directly from the story and only indirectly from the film's production crew. Learning how a movie is made is its own separate story about human creativity and innovation. It can add a fascinating layer to a great film, but it neither adds to nor detracts from the actual story being told.

With a literary lens, truth is transmitted through the

story itself, which is why so many stories can be translated not only from language to language but from medium to medium. The story from a book can be told as a play, as a film, through animation or live action, even as a song. Further, each of those different media probably has different people shaping the way the story is told in that genre. And, if you have a great story, each retelling expands the original story's truth in new and often unexpected ways.

When we are wearing our story glasses, learning about the disputes and "agendas" involved in the creation of the canon or finding out about the difficulties of translation, copying, and transmitting the biblical manuscripts are no longer faith-shaking moments. In fact, they make it all the more amazing that the truths of the Bible still speak as loudly as they do. What seems like an argument against God's hand when seen in a legal context can actually end up being an argument *in favor of* divine inspiration when you look through the story lens.

If the Bible is story, there are no more crises or false choices when you learn how it came to be. With your story lenses, you can have faith *and* scholarship, religion *and* science, and the loving community of your past can be expanded rather than threatened by your new understandings. That's what story does. It's an inviting flame, bringing others closer to the campfire to hear as you tell stories about that wild time you thought a raccoon was your cat and gave it free rein in your house.

So, Did God Inspire the Bible or Not?

The concept of divine inspiration for the Bible is an assertion that can't be proven or disproven. I say yes; you say no. Since we can't prove (or disprove) even the *existence* of God, we certainly can't prove God's inspiration of the Bible. You either take it on faith or you don't. But, now that we're wearing our story glasses, do we really need to duke it out? The question of inspiration becomes a secondary rather than a primary question.

In any discipline, the truth of something doesn't change according to a person's belief or disbelief about it. The law of gravity works whether you believe Isaac Newton's theory or whether you insist that giant cave trolls live in the center of the earth holding really big magnets. Whether you believe gravity is a law of physics or is caused by a bunch of cave trolls will matter if you apply to work for NASA; but if you jump off a building, your beliefs will not affect the outcome. The effect of gravity is the same, no matter how bonkers your explanation for its existence may be.

In the same way, when a Bible story rings true for

someone, that happens irrespective of whether they believe that God wrote it verbatim in the King James English, that God inspired a human author to write the narrative, or that a person created it out of whole cloth without so much as a nudge from a divine actor. A child who has run away from home, gotten into trouble, and found themselves longing to return can relate to Jesus's parable of the Prodigal Son, even if that child is an atheist. The core benefit of a story doesn't lie in where it came from.

Neither the existence of God nor God's involvement in bringing us the Bible is determined by poll results. God is or isn't, inspired the Bible or didn't, no matter what we think. It might be fun to debate on a Saturday night with our beverage of choice, but the question won't be settled at the end. We can prove that the stories of the Bible were created and recorded; we can have at least educated guesses about when they were first told and what community of people may have first shaped and transmitted them. But no one can prove or disprove God's involvement in all that behind the scenes.

With that in mind, we could argue that the question of God's inspiration in the creation of the Bible matters little. The truth is in the story, in allowing the Bible to be a source of wisdom for anyone and everyone, regardless of their religious beliefs. My honors thesis in college was titled "Christian Doctrinal Elements in Norse Mythology."

I don't worship the Norse pantheon, and I wasn't equivocating my Christian faith. I was simply pointing out that truth turns up in the darnedest places, and you don't have to subscribe to a particular faith system to see it. Stories can transcend religious boundaries.

If you think about it, that's actually a fair way for God to do business. Story makes truth accessible to anyone and everyone. It's not gated behind a church door, a checkbook, a certain age, or a particular educational requirement. People who originally heard Jesus tell his stories didn't have to believe he was God or plumb the depths of Jewish theology in order to find life-altering truth. They just followed him around, soaked it up, and went away hopeful, healed, and changed. They might have been rich or poor, slave or free, Jew or Greek, male or female—the stories did not discriminate. It's one of the reasons that those in power found Jesus so threatening. Telling stories allowed him to do an end-run around the power structures and barriers to bring his message directly to the people.

What the stories of Jesus highlight is not so much the importance of the *original* source of a story, but rather the power given to the *immediate* source of the story—in other words, the storyteller. Every story has at least one architect who shaped it and launched it into the world, and we often judge the character of that source by the effect of the story on those who hear it. But once the story has been launched, every subsequent telling shapes the story in some new way, and sometimes the re-telling goes so far afield that the original intent is lost. This is sometimes accidental, sometimes purposeful, and sometimes malevolent. As any trial lawyer can tell you, stories can be told in ways that either reveal or conceal the truth.

The stories of the Bible haven't been immune to those impacts, and in the next chapter we'll look at the power dynamics involved in who is allowed to tell the stories of the Bible and to what ends. But I raise the issue here because we don't usually step back and think about whether a gut reaction we have to a biblical story is a result of the story itself or of the storyteller—whether we've been manipulated in some way or other. If we need to know whether God inspired the stories of the Bible, we have to ask that question not just about those who originally told them, but also about every single person who has told them since. And then we've looped back to a legal lens that tries to define which of those storytellers were "correct."

All that makes my brain hurt. To move forward, let's frame the question differently. On the one hand, if you're a Christian, it's almost necessary that you believe God had some hand in shaping the Bible. After all, it's the Bible that shapes the image of God we believe in, the form of our worship, and our relationship to each other and to our world. So "Did God inspire the Bible?" isn't really a question for Christians. In many ways it's a given. And, on the other hand, it's not really a question for those who don't believe in God, either. They may find wisdom in the Bible, but they would hardly credit that wisdom to a deity whose existence they question. Those of other religions would likewise have to answer the question according to the tenets of their own belief. "Did God inspire the Bible?" isn't the most helpful question. It divides us and sends us scurrying to our own ideological corners.

Fully Human and Fully God

The more fruitful question might be, "Does the Bible spring from a divine or a human source?" To examine that, we need our story lens. The truth of a story is less like a chemical formula and more like a living organism that draws nourishment from many sources at once. And, when we look at it that way, we see that again we have a false choice. Stories don't have to be either divine or human in their source. They can be both.

If the Bible springs from both a divine *and* a human source, then all sides can feast at the same table. The religious call truth "God," and the non-religious call truth "wisdom." But, as with the law of gravity, it doesn't matter what you believe about the nature of the source: the effect is the same. We all come away changed. And if both the religious and the non-religious can connect to the Bible, it's worth considering whether that might be a reflection of a profound combination of divine mystery and human effort.

The Bible doesn't explicitly tell us about its own nature, but it is chock full of stories about the nature of God. Within the Bible we have clues about how God communicates. And that, in turn, might tell us what sort of communication the Bible itself might be. So let's bring this theory to the pages of Scripture: Is the notion that the Bible is both human and divine an idea that the Bible itself supports? Does the God of the Bible operate that way? When God needs to communicate in the Bible, how is it done? What methods does God employ to get a message across?

As you might expect, God can be very creative. In the book of Daniel, we see God communicating through dreams, visions, angels, the inertia of hungry lions, and literally writing on the wall. In other places God communicates through prophets, talking donkeys, stone tablets, the weather, and the voices of regular people sharing experiences with each other. The communication with some is direct, and with others it's indirect. Sometimes it's active; sometimes it's passive. When these instances are taken together, God's "method" for communicating in the Bible seems to be "whatever the person receiving it needs in order to understand and use the information."

That last point is important. God doesn't communicate just for fun or to put on a show. God doesn't jump out of the bushes, shout "Boo!," and then run back to heaven giggling. When God has something to say in the Bible, it's because intervention is necessary to make something happen—to steer the events of human history in the direction God wants. It is purposeful communication. When God speaks in the Bible—whether through dreams or donkeys—it's because a change in course is warranted. Action above and beyond the usual day-to-day activity is needed.

Think about the implications of that for a moment. In theory, God could just make something happen. That ability comes with God's job description. But, if you look at the stories in the Bible, that doesn't seem to be how God usually works. Let's start with an Old Testament example. Presumably the God who created the heavens and the earth could manage a boat. God certainly was in possession of the construction details—we get to read them in all their geeky detail in Genesis 6. But God doesn't pull back curtain number two to reveal a giant ark. God tells Noah to build it, cubit by cubit.

Similar Old Testament examples are abundant. In Exodus, God doesn't put all of Egypt in a freeze frame so that the Hebrew slaves can cut and run. Instead, God uses Moses. Of course, Moses is backed up by miracles, but even the miracles require human participation. The Red

Sea doesn't just open up for the fleeing Israelites to cross. Moses has to literally hold his staff up to part the sea and then again to close it. Just a few chapters later, God helps Israel win a battle, but only if Moses holds up his hands. When his arms get tired and he lets them drop, the enemy starts winning. So, does God give Moses superpowers to continue to hold his arms in the air throughout the battle? Nope. Two other people have to hold his arms up for him. Manna does fall directly from heaven, but it doesn't appear in the Israelites' soup bowls. They have to go out and collect it. Daily.

When Elijah is exhausted and starving, ravens are sent to feed him, and when God wants to resurrect a widow's son, God sends Elijah to make it happen. Even when God writes directly on the wall in Belshazzar's royal palace, it's in a language no one understands and requires human interpretation—from Daniel. When danger looms, God doesn't warn the people directly with a booming voice from heaven. God tells a prophet to tell the people, often with some very weird props.

The New Testament is no different. In fact, the work of God that lies at the center of all of Christianity—the saving of the world through Jesus—is done, well, *through* Jesus—by God *in the flesh*, living as a human being within human history. The entire point of all of the New Testament is that for the work of God to be done in the world, it takes both the human and the divine working together. In fact, the only Bible stories I can think of where there's no earthly agent used to bring about the desired result are the creation of the world (where there literally were no earthly agents to do it) and the resurrection of Jesus. None of the other stories imply that God is powerless to act. The Bible simply describes a God who prefers not to act alone.

When Elijah is exhausted and starving, ravens are sent to feed him, and when God wants to resurrect a widow's son, God sends Elijah to make it happen. Even when God writes directly on the wall in Belshazzar's royal palace, it's in a language no one understands and requires human interpretation—from Daniel. When danger looms, God doesn't warn the people directly with a booming voice from heaven. God tells a prophet to tell the people, often with some very weird props.

It's not a limited God that we hear about; it's a self-limited God who works in and through the people and creatures of the earth. A mother bird weakens her young if she breaks open their eggs to help them get out. She watches over them, keeping them warm and protected, as they build the strength they need to survive. The God described in the Bible appears to do the same—the divine and the mortal, working together.

Incarnation

In the biblical stories, God did intervene directly from time to time. But by far the most common way that the people in the Bible experienced God and heard God's message was in and through other human beings. Given that, it might be worth our while to put aside questions about the Bible's "inspiration" and talk instead about "incarnation." In theological terms, incarnation is exactly what Christians believe God did in Jesus. God at work—in human flesh, in human history. Fully human and fully God. Jesus was not some factoid dropped from the sky. God's truth became a human being, and that truth became known through relationships that were forged in the stories of a people.

When the characters of the Bible wanted to find God, they didn't look up into the sky. They looked to other people—to prophets, priests, and kings; to teachers and to their ancestors' stories. And sometimes they still missed God's presence because they thought a poor baby in a manger or the words of mere shepherds were a bit too earthy for the glory of God. When the Pharisees asked Jesus where to look for God's kingdom, Jesus responded, "The kingdom of God is not coming with things that can be observed; nor will they say, 'Look, here it is!' or 'There it is!' For, in fact, the kingdom of God is among you" (Luke 17:20–21).

So, it turns out that the Bible *does* tell us how it is to be read and approached. We are encouraged to approach the Word made words (i.e., the Bible) in exactly the same way that we approach the Word made flesh in Jesus—as we are, where we are, in relationship with each other. Wise as serpents and innocent as doves. Human and divine together. In relationships, and in the wise stories that forge them, this mortal flesh puts on immortality. Both the Bible and Jesus can be—indeed, must be—fully human and fully God.

When the characters of the Bible wanted to find God, they didn't look up into the sky. They looked to other people—to prophets, priests, and kings; to teachers and to their ancestors' stories. And sometimes they still missed God's presence because they thought a poor baby in a manger or the words of mere shepherds were a bit too earthy for the glory of God.

This doesn't mean that the Bible contains distinctly human and divine elements and that some knowing person can distinguish which is which. But, just like the Christian doctrine about the nature of Jesus, God's revelation in the Bible is both at once, giving both those who seek human wisdom and those who seek divine inspiration a way to find themselves in its pages. The very first chapter of Genesis tells us that God made human beings—both male and female—in the image of God (Gen.

1:27). Every one of us is that mix of the divine image and human limitation, and there's no way to pull them apart from each other, although we often try. That mix is foundational to creation and achieves its perfection in Christ. The Bible is yet another revelation of that human and divine combination.

As Christians, we find it natural to see all of God's revelation as fundamentally the same—in creation, in the Bible, and in Jesus. And it rings "true" because of the positive effect on our lives such a view can produce. If Jesus is fully human and fully divine, then maybe the next time I encounter a homeless addict, I'll be more likely to see both the human need and the divine spark that calls me to wrap a towel around my waist and serve. If the Bible is fully human and fully divine, then maybe when I encounter a challenging story I can see both the folly of mortals and the breath of God trying to bring forth new life in the desert of human experience.

CHAPTER 4

Re-viewing Power

The Influence of the Storyteller

What then is freedom? The power to live as one wishes.

—Cicero

Power, according to the dictionary, is simply the ability to act. It's not a giant monster to be conquered, nor are those who seek it evil. On the flip side, those without power are not lesser human beings. Power—the ability to act—is simply another way of describing freedom, making it not just any human right, but perhaps the most fundamental of them all. A healthy use of power is necessary for any relationship to thrive, whether between friends, family, states, or nations. But that is no easy task.

To achieve the Bible's vision of a just and peaceful world, we need certain restraints on our exercise of power. It's the age-old paradox that to have any degree of practical freedom, some of our freedom must be limited by law. I'm not really free to leave my house if my neighbor is free to shoot me without consequence if I do so. My freedom to drive on the highway and arrive safely at my destination is dependent on a civic agreement that we will all obey the laws of the road. But the delicate dance of law and freedom is easily corrupted; and the relationship between the Bible and structures of power has a long and difficult history, especially when the power of the Bible has been joined to the power of the state.

The Bible is an extremely powerful book in its own right, exerting various kinds of power over different groups of people. But Bibles don't jump up off the shelf and act on their own. The power of a story isn't activated until it is told, and, like a knife that can help someone either cut the carrots or slit your throat, the impact of the Bible's incredible power is determined by the intent, skill, and knowledge of the one who wields it. Because of that, it's important to look at three primary things: The power of the biblical narratives as a whole, the issues surrounding who has the power to shape those stories for public consumption, and what the stories of the Bible themselves teach us about the use of power.

The Power of Connection

The stories of the Bible are powerful across both time and culture in part because they are stories rooted in universal human experience. They are stories of families and nations, love and war, success and failure, sinners and saints. Hollywood loves these stories for precisely that reason. Greed and betrayal, honor and sacrifice, sibling rivalry and treachery, bigotry and slavery—they form the stuff of human life today just as they did then. It's easy to see ourselves and our world in them.

We also relate because the metaphors for biblical teaching are so frequently earthy and organic. Sometimes we're the farmer sowing seed, and sometimes we're the grain being sifted; sometimes we're the arborist pruning branches, and sometimes we're the tree planted by streams of water. Jesus is the vine, and we are the branches; Israel is the fig tree, and we are the sheep—or sometimes the goats. In the Bible, the earth we all inhabit becomes our teacher, giving universal access to its lessons.

Those common connections are a powerful draw in and of themselves, but that strength is dwarfed by the power of hope that frames and drives them. While there are many parts of the Bible that can hardly be called hopeful, they are but scenes from a much larger story. Woven through that grand story is a glimmering thread of hope, which proclaims that after exile will be return, after sin will be forgiveness, after death will be life. Sometimes that thread of hope is in the foreground, and sometimes it's hidden in the background; but you always know that it's there. It's the entire premise of the Bible: A loving God is always at work in the world for good.

> *While there are many parts of the Bible that can hardly be called hopeful, they are but scenes from a much larger story. Woven through that grand story is a glimmering thread of hope, which proclaims that after exile will be return.*

Even those of us who hold to that belief question it in the dark times; but that is exactly why we go back to the well of the Bible—to have our hope renewed. And its stories do not fail, because in them we find characters just like ourselves. Even Jesus used the words of the psalmist to ask why God had forsaken him. When even the most faithful characters of the Bible fall into despair—Elijah, Jeremiah, Jesus—we know the Bible "gets us." When the pain and sorrows of the human condition are then woven into stories threaded with hope, the thread becomes a rope we cling to for our lives. And hope is power.

The Bible is also powerful because it is revered by so many. Well over half of the Christian Bible is comprised of the sacred text of the Jews. The seeds of those stories grow differently in the unique soil of each religion, but they connect Jews and Christians in profound ways. Likewise, Muslims look to many of the biblical stories for wisdom and the voice of God. Again, the plants that spring from those seeds are different, both in the details of the stories and in their interpretation, but they serve as a point of connection. There's a reason that Christians, Jews, and Muslims are all called "People of the Book."

In August of 2016, the world's population was 7.4 billion. Of those, 2.2 billion are Christians, 1.6 billion are Muslims, and 16 million are Jews. Add up those figures, and you have over half the world's population connected in a deep way to an overlapping set of stories in the Bible. Now add the impact the Bible has had on Western culture more generally. The influence of the Bible can be found in every single one of the arts, the English language, our systems of democracy, and the debates in the public square. If you live in the West, the Bible is in your life whether you want it there or not. And, with the efforts of missionaries and global communication networks, I challenge you to find a spot anywhere in the world where there's not at least a glimpse of biblical influence. It might be welcome, or it might be resented, but it's there—a near universal infrastructure at the ready. Access is also power.

Nuclear power can be used for creation or destruction, depending on the intent of the ones who use it. Similarly, the power of the Bible can be used for great good, but history has shown it can also be manipulated for devastating harm. We might embrace the Bible, view it as an odd curiosity, or shun it in good conscience; but to be ignorant of it or dismissive of its power can endanger us all if we don't pay attention to who is harnessing and distributing that power and why. Never take your eye off the storyteller.

Controlling the Story:
The Danger of Joining Church and State

Show me a good storyteller, and I will show you a leader. Story is the stuff of life, so those who can weave events into compelling stories will never fail to gain a following. But not all compelling stories are helpful. Stories of racial superiority have created atrocity. Stories told by radical religious leaders have resulted in hate crimes and terrorism. Stories told by the media have brought down governments. The way to tell a good story from a bad one is not by whether it's compelling, but rather by the effect it has on those who apply the story to their lives. Or, as Jesus put it, "You will know them by their fruits" (Matt. 7:16).

Those responsible for telling stories in public—politicians, film directors, journalists, teachers, songwriters, pastors, writers, and so on—are shaping those who listen;

and that means you. Get a big enough audience for your stories, and the reality of a nation and even the world can shift. Every tyrant knows this almost instinctively, which is why they always go after the press, teachers, artists, and writers. To control a people, you must have complete control of the story, whether you're an authoritarian dictator banning books or a media corporation buying up all the outlets. Which is exactly why history is full of attempts to control the story of the Bible and press it into service of the government.

From the fourth century, when Constantine adopted the Christian faith and made it the official religion of the Roman Empire, and continuing right to the morning news, the Bible has been at the center of both tyranny and its resistance in the West. The battles over who has access to the stories of the Bible have engulfed kings and dictators, popes and martyrs for two thousand years. Those who have sought to put the text of the Bible into the hands of all people, setting the stories free to live and breathe through every person able to pick up the book and read it, have almost universally been seen as subversive. As of this writing, you can be imprisoned or killed for owning a Bible in North Korea, the Maldives, Morocco, Libya, and Uzbekistan. But, lest we blame it on other faiths and languages, let's look quickly at the history of the suppression of the Bible in English by

Christians. For the sake of brevity, we'll just go back to the Middle Ages.

At the Council of Toulouse in 1229, the church officially forbade the laity to read vernacular translations of the Bible—in any language. If you were found with such a translation, you were subject to the Inquisition. Those who created such translations were labeled heretics and often martyred. It wasn't long before owning a translation of the Bible wasn't just heresy in the church but also outlawed by the state. But the Bible is powerful. It would not be suppressed, and after a few hundred years of trying, the governments of Europe decided it would be easier to embrace the Bible and do their own "authorized" translations, making sure that word choice and any sidebar notes were supportive of their cause. Henry VIII did it in England with the Great Bible in 1539; John Calvin did it in Geneva in 1560; and then, most famously, King James of England did it in 1611. And just like the nations themselves, those Bibles duked it out for control of hearts and minds. Finally, a hundred years after the publication of the King James Bible and five hundred years after the Council of Toulouse forbade the reading of the Bible by laity, Pope Clement XI declared, "The reading of Sacred Scripture is for all."

But allowing anyone to read the Bible and allowing anyone to interpret it are two different things. From Constantine onwards, church and state were joined at the hip

in most of the West. To challenge the authorized interpretation of the Bible was to challenge the power of the
state, a lethal combination. Religious persecution raged,
eventually bringing a ship called the *Mayflower* to American shores. My own ancestors were on that ship.

Unfortunately, when the *Mayflower* passengers established the Massachusetts Bay Colony, they quickly for-
got their own story and made the exact same mistake in
America. Their establishment of their own interpretation
of the Bible as the rule of law gave us the Salem witch trials
and the persecution of other forms of Christian faith. Others of my ancestors had to flee from Cape Cod to Rhode
Island because their Quaker beliefs were not welcome in
Massachusetts Bay. Baptist minister Roger Williams fled
as well, founding Rhode Island with the strong conviction
that church and state must remain distinct and separate
entities. In 1644, in *The Bloudy Tenent of Persecution for Cause
of Conscience*, he wrote,

> An enforced uniformity of religion throughout a nation
> or civil state, confounds the civil and religious, denies
> the principles of Christianity and civility, and that Jesus
> Christ has come in the flesh.

Over a hundred years later, the founders of the United
States agreed and made the separation of church and state

foundational to our democracy. Our constitution says we may not establish a religion for the state or forbid the people the right to live out their religious beliefs. Constitutionally, the Bible can be utilized by our people but not usurped by our leaders. Having unfettered access to the Bible and the power of its stories is a freedom for which people have died across several continents for more than a thousand years.

To many, that freedom—the power to choose that particular set of stories and apply them without coercion in our lives—seems unimportant; it's just a relic of an unenlightened time that's unworthy of secular support or protection. But extreme brands of Christian faith, now growing in power and influence in the United States and elsewhere, believe the government again should have ultimate control over the stories of the Bible and wield the text as a legal document with a mandate for all. When the Bible is presented as a law to be followed instead of a story to be lived, that's a red flag we ignore at our peril. Remember: Never take your eyes off the storyteller.

> *Constitutionally, the Bible can be utilized by our people but not usurped by our leaders. Having unfettered access to the Bible and the power of its stories is a freedom for which people have died across several continents for more than a thousand years.*

Dominion and Power: In the Beginning

Since power is defined as the freedom to act, asking what the Bible teaches about power is really asking what the Bible teaches about human behavior and interaction. The stories we find in Scripture address many specific behaviors, from the broad strokes of loving your neighbor all the way down to how many loops should be sewn into the tabernacle curtains. But when we pull back to the balcony view of the grand themes that infuse these stories, the guiding principles for the use of human power are clear; and we get them in the very first stories of the Bible.

It starts with two distinct accounts of creation in Genesis 1 and 2. They differ in style, content, and most likely in origin, but they appear back to back for a reason: Each gives a unique but related view of God's nature and human purpose. The two stories aren't meant to be harmonized, but neither are they meant to be seen apart from one another. If you try to read them like a textbook, you'll be twisted in knots and fail your science classes. (This isn't God trying to be your geology professor.) But if you read them as the opening chapters of a larger story, each with its own point about a common set of truths, the message flows together and connects the accounts to each other, to the chapters that follow, and, ultimately, to the Bible as a whole.

The epic, highly structured poem of Genesis 1 shows us that all existence is derived from a God who prefers order to chaos and exercises power for good. Unlike other creation stories from the ancient Near East, Genesis 1 offers no grand battles between multiple gods, no body parts used to make the heavens and earth, no winners and losers. In the Bible, we watch in awe as the power of the word, not the power of the sword, creates order out of chaos, and caps it all off with God's pronouncement that it is "good."

In addition, Genesis 1 doesn't just tell us about God; it also gives us a critical piece of information about humanity:

> So God created humankind in his image, in the image of God he created them; male and female he created them. God blessed them, and God said to them, "Be fruitful and multiply, and fill the earth and subdue it; and have dominion over the fish of the sea and over the birds of the air and over every living thing that moves upon the earth." (Gen. 1:27–28)

God makes people—both men and women—in God's own image and then places them in charge of the newly created world. The power given to humans here is called "dominion," which is where I'd like to pause. The word "dominion" here isn't a problem if we're reading a story, because we know this is just the first chapter. Stories build over time, and tidbits dropped in Chapter 1 get fleshed out as we go along. The story reader says, "Hmmm ... dominion ... I wonder what God means by that?" and goes on to Chapter 2 to learn more.

But those who are reading with a legal eye take a different approach. Those expecting the Bible to provide law can't move on until everything is clearly defined. They parse every word carefully, the way a lawyer would examine a legal contract. What does this word mean? Are there loopholes? What exactly can I do here? When applied to this passage of Scripture, the legal lens sees the word "dominion," pulls out a dictionary, and decides, "Yup. We have the power. We can do what we want with the earth. God intends for us to use its resources according to our needs and desires."

A legal reader first determines the exact meaning of the first passage and then interprets subsequent passages in light of what has come before. A story reader picks up clues about meaning and moves forward until the whole picture takes shape. Genesis 1 left us story readers wondering how we should understand this "dominion" gift. The legal readers are still back there, trying to figure it out. The story readers have moved on to Chapter 2 and are now gaining clarity: "The LORD God took the man and put him in the Garden of Eden to till it and keep it." Aha! "Dominion" means we're the keepers, not the owners, of the earth, and to "subdue" means to tend it as a gardener would keep an orchard for the one who planted it.

As we join Adam in the continuing story, we discover that God can curtail or even revoke our "dominion" if certain conditions aren't met. As it turns out, this dominion thing doesn't even let you eat all the fruit! Adam and Eve rebel against those limits and try to take full control by eating the forbidden fruit. But when they abandon their role as keepers and try to do as they please, their world becomes a much more inhospitable place. Death looms on the horizon. By Genesis 4, their eldest son has killed his brother. The story expands our understanding of "dominion" yet again as we learn that we're not just the keepers of the earth; we're also meant to be our "brother's keeper." As we feel the guilt of Cain and the grief of his parents, we discover that what we have subdued in our grasp for ultimate power is ourselves.

However diverse their origins might be, these early chapters form a single story that establishes the Bible's view of the created order and the role human beings are meant to play within it. It's not a legal text to be parsed, and it's not a science textbook trying to establish the age of the earth. It's a story that sets the stage for all the stories that follow with a reminder that if we usurp God's power or misuse the power given to us, all of our relationships, including with the earth itself, will suffer the consequences.

But the story that begins in a garden in Genesis doesn't end there. It goes on to remind us that when we forget, there is always One who remembers. When we're lost, there is always One out seeking for us. And when we find ourselves longing for home, there is One who will take us back to a new heaven and a new earth, with a new garden to tend. Because that's what real power does: It protects and it serves to create a blessing for all nations. It goes last even when it could rightfully claim first place. It dies so that others might live. Christians won't fully understand "dominion" until we have followed the story to a cross.

> But the story that begins in a garden in Genesis doesn't end there. It goes on to remind us that when we forget, there is always One who remembers. When we're lost, there is always One out seeking for us. And when we find ourselves longing for home, there is One who will take us back to a new heaven and a new earth, with a new garden to tend.

CHAPTER 5

Focus on the Promise

....

Moving from Fear to Hope

There is no hope unmingled with fear, and no fear unmingled with hope.

—Baruch Spinoza

At first blush you might think hope is good and fear is bad, but that's not how it works. Imagine that your life is like a car. If you're going to take that car out on the road, you had better have two things: an accelerator and a good set of brakes. In one sense the two are opposites: the accelerator makes the car go faster, and the brakes slow it down or even bring it to a complete stop if necessary. But you can't go to the car lot and find some cars with only brakes or others with only gas pedals. We need them both to drive safely.

It's the same with hope and fear. For many Christians,

it's tempting to see the fearful stories in Scripture as somehow less valuable than those that focus on hope. Hope feels better, and, in stories as in life, we prefer to push painful feelings to one side. But hope is the gas pedal and fear is the brake as we take the car of our lives out onto the road. Each has more or less of a role to play, depending on the situation around us. If the stories of the Bible are to be of any earthly help to us, they need to be true to the lives we live; and those lives include times of fear and threat.

Any story we read has real peril for its characters. Even Winnie the Pooh had to deal with rising floodwaters and strained relationships. Those anxious parts of the story are critical to the overall message. You can hardly be declared a brave hero if you've never faced any danger. If we see the Bible as something that can be pulled apart into a variety of stand-alone passages, it's easy just to pull out the hopeful ones and pretend that the fearful sections are the product of some less-enlightened age. But if the Bible is story, taking out the chapters that disturb us makes the overall plot almost unintelligible. The meta-story of Scripture promises that we're traveling a road that will take us from fear to hope. There's no way to understand how we arrive at that promise apart from experiencing the whole journey from start to finish. And what a journey it is.

Snakes on a Pole

There are some very odd stops along that biblical road, and the one in Numbers 21 is so weird that Christians would probably ignore it entirely if Jesus hadn't mentioned it. Many ignore it even so. But stories make less sense if you skip chapters, so I want to stop in this tiny town to illustrate how the story lens can bring this odd tale into focus. If you look out the window, you'll see that the Israelites are wandering in the wilderness, making their way from slavery in Egypt to freedom in the Promised Land. It's been a while, and they've gotten a bit testy. And who can blame them? Life in the desert is hot and harsh. Not surprisingly, their complaints have gotten louder and louder. They grumble openly now at both Moses and God, wondering aloud whether remaining slaves in Egypt might not have been the better option.

But God would like a bit more gratitude. After all, God's done some amazing things: sent a ton of impressive plagues, orchestrated the whole Red Sea miracle, arranged manna and quail to literally drop from the sky for them to eat, and given them the constant guidance of a cloud by day and a pillar of fire by night. And the capper? A promised land flowing with milk and honey awaits them at their destination. All that should count for something. But it doesn't. So, after one whine too many, God gets mad and sends them poisonous snakes. The snakes cause the Israelites to adjust their attitudes, and they cry out to Moses for help and healing. He pleads their case before God, who gives Moses a decidedly odd solution. Moses is to make a serpent of bronze and put it up on a pole. Everyone who looks at it will be healed.

If you're reading this story with textbook lenses, you'll be disappointed with the medicinal value of such an object. The anti-venom at your local ER will work better. If you put on legal glasses, they'll frame the story in terms of a rebellious people questioning God's judgment, then receiving a just punishment followed by a gift of healing that they didn't deserve. That lens makes better sense than a magical, healing snake on a pole, but it does paint a rather grim image of a God who'll drop poisonous snakes on you if you question God's timing or agenda. Roll up the window, will you?

But what about story? Suppose this is but one scene in the story of the Exodus from Egypt, which is itself part of the larger drama of the creation of the nation of Israel, which is a microcosm of the journey of the entire people of God from bondage to freedom—from fear to hope. What then? Story invites us to join the journey. From within the story, we can see the hardships and dangers of our own wilderness. We experience with the Israelites their frustrations and fears that the promise can't be realized right away. We see ourselves in them and cry out to God with them. And we are taught, as they are, that in order to become whole, we have to look square in the eyes of the very thing that terrifies us, ask for help, and acknowledge any parts of it that we've brought upon ourselves. If you think about it, it's the first seven steps of every twelve-step program on the planet, all rolled into one snake on a pole.

With our story lenses, we also know instinctively that this isn't the whole picture, but just one piece of many we've collected along the way. In fact, if we got into this story at the beginning, we might notice that we picked up a similar piece much, much earlier. This isn't the first time a snake has brought us death. As we look at the snake on the pole in Numbers, a garden memory of a crafty serpent near some forbidden fruit takes shape. That snake gave us very bad advice, and, just like now, death was the result. We look at the bronze serpent again. Is *that* what we have to acknowledge for our healing? And what does it all mean? Well, it's still relatively early in the story. We now know to put the new piece in our pack with the others and let the story unfold.

The expectation of an unfolding narrative makes us less likely to scratch our heads when, in the middle of Jesus's famous discussion with Nicodemus about being "born again," Jesus says, "Just as Moses lifted up the serpent in the wilderness, so must the Son of Man be lifted up, that whoever believes in him may have eternal life." Say what? Of all the amazing stories Jesus could reference, he picks that one? If we aren't reading the Bible as story, we're lost. But if we've jumped in and gotten to know the characters, if we've ridden with them on the road from the very beginning, we slap our hand to our forehead and say, "Of course!"

This new piece provides the climax for the story, which might go something like this. Listening to the snake in the Garden led to death, and we became slaves to its power. To be healed of that mortal wound, we had to face what we had done by looking at a snake on a pole and admit we couldn't heal ourselves. With that ritual in place, we can leave the wilderness and live our lives until the day when we find ourselves at the foot of Calvary's Tree.

This time, when we look death in the eye, we see that Jesus's body on the pole of the Cross has created a portal with a glimpse of a garden on the other side. If we join Jesus on that tree, if we take up our own cross and follow, we can reverse that early curse and be born again into eternal life. Death is swallowed up in victory; streams break forth in the desert; our mourning is turned to dancing. And a little child can play on the nest of an adder without fear.

It's Getting Hot in Here: Braking for Hell

Meanwhile, back on Earth-1, we are again in the car, and the author of Hebrews is blaring on the radio: "It is a fearsome thing to fall into the hands of the living God." This message comes through loud and clear in both the Old and the New Testament. The Bible tells us in Proverbs that "The fear of the LORD is the beginning of wisdom." But the Bible is equally clear that, while such fear might be the *beginning* of wisdom, it is not wisdom's end. We are also told, just pages away from the end of the whole thing, "There is no fear in love, but perfect love casts out all fear" (1 John 4:18). That's where the road ultimately leads—perfect love—and that promised destination makes it worth the drive.

Before that point of perfection, however, the stories of the Bible remind us that fear is still a relevant and even necessary part of a faithful life—although we note that fear is supposed to be a check against bad behavior, not the motivator for doing what's right. And, as our story continues, the balance for the faithful should be gradually shifting away from fear and toward the fulfillment of our hope in love. Fear will enter our lives from time to time, but we're not supposed to drive through life riding the brakes. The Bible never, ever suggests that a faithful life should be a fearful life; and all of the stories in its pages—even the frightening ones—are meant to be seen in the context of the central promise of both the Old and the New Testament together: If you find yourself in exile, there will come a time to return; if you find yourself dead, a resurrection awaits, because a loving God is with us. The biblical balance is always heavily weighted toward hope and promise.

Riding the fear brake is a temptation we must learn to overcome, and part of that learning is realizing that fear is an emotion common to us all. It is in some ways our human condition and, when seen in that universal light, can lead us toward one another. That is the role fear is supposed to play. It warns us of danger, slows us down so that we can check our direction, and leads us to seek help from each other. The fearful sections of Scripture are part of the much larger story about the journey of our lives. We might enter the wilderness at different times and places in our lives, but it comes to us all, and that common experience of difficult and anxious days draws us together. It is no longer my story or yours. It is our story—the human story—and the Bible can't be our story without it.

Unfortunately, any powerful emotion can be weaponized, and fear is a favorite in the arsenal of evil. There are

> *The biblical balance is always heavily weighted toward hope and promise.*

those who take the frightening parts of the Bible out of the bigger story and read them to you as a judge might read you an indictment. The legal lens weaponizes the fear, implying that it doesn't apply to all of us—just to you, the unwashed heathen. You, the criminal. You, the sinner. Not them, not us—you. Viewing stories as law divides us from one another. That lens not only threatens us with hell—it places us there immediately by isolating us in our fear. Gone is the sense of our human community navigating the desert together. Instead, it's just you in your car, in a ditch, with the sense that it's all your fault.

The doctrine of hell as expressed by the hellfire-and-damnation preacher is a detour that will throw our cars off a cliff. In the context of the grand narrative of the Bible—that journey from fear to hope—we expect to encounter the wilderness along the way. We expect to make a wrong turn or two; there might even be snakes. But we also have been assured that the story which brought us into that desert will also lead us out. That's the promise. The bullying threat of eternal torment rips that story from our hands and tries to tell us that if we make one wrong turn, we'll never get back on the right road. Go that way, and God will not seek us out and lead us home but instead will order our eternal destruction. In fact, we're actually on that hell-bent road even if we're feeling pretty good about our life. On that journey we're either going to be riding those brakes for the rest of our lives, or hitting the gas and getting to another story as fast as is humanly possible.

The idea of an actual place of eternal, fiery torture for unrepentant and wicked souls requires that we view the Bible as a legal text meant to be taken literally. As we've seen with other issues, the legal and factual approaches can cause both conflict and distortion of the Bible's message. When applied to the notion of hell, a literal reading can give license to commit atrocity. Think about it. If it's okay for God to sentence people to eternal torture, then any human punishment has trouble ever rising to the standard of "cruel and inhumane." With that belief in our arsenal, we can justify pretty much anything done to those convicted of a crime. Ironically, this makes atrocity even more likely in a "Christian" penal system than in a secular one.

Preaching that divides us from one another and moves people in the opposite direction of hope might be supported in isolated texts as viewed through a legal or literal lens, but it's not the story of the Bible as a whole. It's not, in short, gospel. The word "gospel" means "good news." Screaming "You're going to hell and will burn forever!" is a rather twisted definition of "good news." And yet, I've heard it a million times: "God loves you sooooo much that God sent his only Son to die for you. Why, even if you were the only person on earth, Jesus would still have come to die for your sins. God loves you—yes, you—that much. And if you don't believe it, that same loving, generous God is going to open the trap door to hell and let the devil torture you for all eternity."

Not only does that doctrine of hell present us with a God who is nothing like Christians claim; it gives us a picture of the universe that doesn't rise to the level of basic fairness, let alone the justice we like to go on and on about. Even if I sinned from the moment of conception until my dying breath, my sin still would have a beginning and an end. In other words, it would be limited. In what world is unlimited torment a fair punishment for a limited crime? That kind of thinking doesn't even pass the eye-for-an-eye test; and it certainly doesn't come close to "Turn the other cheek." Treating the Bible like a literal and legal text lands us not only in hot water but in a fiery lake.

There and Back Again:
From Hell to Hope in the Book of Romans

What happens if we take off the literal/legal glasses and look at the passages describing hell as story? If they aren't giving us literal *facts*, what bigger *truths* might they be telling us? Well, for starters, they can be telling us that we're not alone, either in our desire for retribution when we are

FOCUS ON THE PROMISE

wronged, or in our abject despair, a state in which we often find ourselves. Like the author of Psalm 137, sometimes we hurt so bad that we want God to smite even the innocent children of our enemies. And sometimes we turn that fear inward and find ourselves in an emotional hell that leaves us paralyzed. Those stories tell us that others have been to those places before us.

Those stories can also reinforce the point that God is just, and that people will be held accountable for their actions. Any number of Jesus's parables tell us this, as well as the entire book of Revelation and much of the Old Testament. Whether we receive this news as frightening or hopeful depends on whether the actions in question are ours or someone else's. If we are among the persecuted, as the believers who received the book of Revelation were, the announcement that angels will pour out bowls of wrath is a hopeful message because it signals that God has indeed heard our cries and there will be justice. On the flip side, if we're thinking about our own failings, these stories can stir the fear that becomes "the beginning of wisdom": There are rules, and there are consequences for breaking them. Oh, and snakes.

That is exactly the fear and frustration Paul is describing in Romans 7. We can't seem to escape the corruption waiting for us at every turn—even when we know it's there and we desperately want to make the right choices. But Paul quickly turns that despair around by reminding us of the larger story. As he proceeds, we can feel the despair lifting with the promise of new life—not just for people, but for all of creation. Through the Spirit, God is with us—in us—and not even death can take that away. By the end of the next chapter, Paul has pulled his readers fully out of that hellish despair and gives us this assurance to keep us from drifting back:

> For I am convinced that neither death, nor life, nor angels, nor rulers, nor things present, nor things to come, nor powers, nor height, nor depth, nor anything else in all creation, will be able to separate us from the love of God in Christ Jesus our Lord. (Rom. 8:38–39)

Romans 8 is full of all kinds of things that theologians like to argue about, and if you read the Bible as a legal text, then by all means, argue away. Plead your case. But if you can give some breathing room to the idea of the book of Romans as literature (which, again, can still be fully God-breathed), then you realize that Romans is like a fifth Gospel. It is Paul, hoping to build a relationship with the church in Rome, telling them the "good news" as he has seen and experienced it. It's his story of the salvation message, combined with his explanation of what that means.

Martin Luther, the Catholic priest who started the Protestant Reformation in the sixteenth century, was caught in exactly the kind of despair Paul describes in Romans. Luther was doing all he could to keep both his actions and his motives pure, but he just couldn't manage it. He was afraid to hit the gas in case he missed atoning for some sin along the way. He was so hard on himself that the priest hearing his confessions finally told him to go out and do something worth confessing! But Luther saw no way out. He had abandoned all hope of his salvation, and his car had slowed to a crawl.

And then one day he read the book of Romans. It wasn't his first rodeo. As a priest, he had read Romans many times before. But this time he really read it; and, as Paul told the story of the human condition in Romans 3, Luther really entered the story for the first time and saw himself: "For no human being will be justified in God's sight" (v. 20). *Exactly*, he thought. It was depressing as hell—literally.

But then came verses 21–24, which turned the whole thing on its head:

> But now, apart from law, the righteousness of God has been disclosed, and is attested by the law and the prophets, the righteousness of God through faith in Jesus Christ for all who believe. For there is no distinction, since all have sinned and fall short of the glory of God; they are now justified by his grace as a gift, through the redemption that is in Christ Jesus.

Luther couldn't believe it. There was a lifeline of hope right in front of his eyes. He couldn't justify himself, but he didn't have to. He had help. There was grace. It had been there all along, in the law, in the prophets—he just was so focused on the fear of his own sinfulness and the consequent judgment that he couldn't see the hope that had been there from the beginning. God isn't a monster waiting to burn him in a fiery hell, he realized. There was grace. And he wasn't alone. Paul had taken the same road he had, and God had still found him, forgiven him, loved him. This realization changed Luther's life, and he hit the gas, heading straight into town to post the news on the church door. There is hope! We're done with the law thing! You don't have to ride the brakes—here, read the story for yourself! It woke all of Europe.

Almost two centuries later, another member of the clergy was in a similar state of despair. John Wesley was an Anglican priest who had just completed a disastrous mission effort in the American colony of Georgia. When he returned to England, Wesley realized that, despite his profession, he really didn't have any faith. It was a sham, and he confessed that lack of faith to a Moravian friend, Peter Böhler. His famous advice to Wesley was to "Preach faith till you have it, and then because you have it, you will preach faith."

It was kind of circular logic, but, to Wesley's amazement, it worked. When he started preaching a faith he didn't really have, his listeners responded and converted. This mystified him, and he began reading his Bible more to see what exactly he had missed. He also had more conversations with Böhler in which he shared his struggles. Then, on a May evening in 1738, at Böhler's urging, he reluctantly attended a religious gathering where someone was reading from—wait for it—Luther's preface to his commentary on Romans. Here's how Wesley described what happened as he listened to Luther's summary of what Romans really meant:

> While he was describing the change which God works in the heart through faith in Christ, I felt my heart strangely warmed. I felt I did trust in Christ, Christ alone for salvation; and an assurance was given me that He had taken away my sins, even mine, and saved me from the law of sin and death.

Just like Luther, Wesley found his life transformed, and, along with his brother Charles, he took England by storm, starting the Methodist movement that accelerated across England and then America, bringing both religious and social reform.

Reading the Bible as law had led both Luther and Wesley to focus on themselves, fear the judgment of God, and finally to abandon all hope because they couldn't keep that law. The Bible wasn't new to either of them. They were both clergy who knew multiple languages and had studied the Bible in great depth. But they were reading the Bible as law and, in doing so, heard a message of condemnation. Despair was the natural result. But when they suddenly saw the Bible not as law, but as the story of a promise, literally everything changed. They sprang up from the hell of their despair, released the brakes, and moved forward quickly and freely into a new hope. It changed their respective worlds.

From Hope to Promise: We are Not Alone

The most common word for "hope" in the Old Testament is the Hebrew word *tiqvah*, which literally means "cord." Hope is the lifeline that, if we cling to it, will pull us out of the hell of despair. And, if there's a lifeline, there must be someone at the other end who threw it to us. If there's a road, then someone has come before us and cleared a path to help us find our way. We are not alone.

Every story in the Bible is meant to be seen in the light of that overarching promise. When Jesus sends his disciples out into the surrounding towns to preach the gospel, the message he tells them to preach is "The kingdom of God has come near to you." That, of course, is where we started in the Garden of Eden, when the presence of God was "among the trees of the garden." And we end our journey in the New Jerusalem, where "the city has no need of sun or moon to shine on it, for the glory of the Lord is its light." No law exists that is separate from that story. Every other promise in Scripture relies on that one, and every fear is mitigated by it: God is with us. Emmanuel.

If there's a road, then someone has come before us and cleared a path to help us find our way. We are not alone. Every story in the Bible is meant to be seen in the light of that overarching promise.

While there are many Christian creeds, both ancient and modern, my all-time favorite is the one from the United Church of Canada, written in 1968. It doesn't try to parse out the exact nature of the Trinity or explain things that are beyond us. It simply proclaims the most fundamental promise of the Bible, thrown out as a lifeline of hope to anyone in despair:

We are not alone,
    we live in God's world.

We believe in God:
    who has created and is creating,

who has come in Jesus,
    the Word made flesh,
    to reconcile and make new,
who works in us and others
    by the Spirit.

We trust in God.

We are called to be the Church:
    to celebrate God's presence,
    to live with respect in Creation,
    to love and serve others,
    to seek justice and resist evil,
    to proclaim Jesus, crucified and risen,
        our judge and our hope.

In life, in death, in life beyond death,
    God is with us.
We are not alone.

    Thanks be to God.

CHAPTER 6

Grinding the Lenses

....

The Story of Suffering

Anything you want to say about God you better make
sure you can say in front of a pit of burning babies.

—Elie Wiesel

In the title of his bestselling book, Rabbi Kushner asked, "Why do bad things happen to good people?" It was a bestselling book because everybody and their grandmother asks that question. And people of faith, especially, would very much like the Bible to answer it for us. And it doesn't. In fact, the Bible *can't* answer that question—at least not in the way that the question is usually posed.

The Bible can't give us an "answer" because the Bible isn't a textbook designed to provide the factual answers to questions. The Bible teaches us, but the teaching isn't presented as a sheet of FAQs that lets us scroll down to questions with answers about the nature of suffering, evil, and the like. The Bible approaches faith and its complex questions by telling us stories, and it is no different when the stories depict violence, anguish, and suffering. Those stories invite us in to remember the times we, too, cried to God in our pain, or perhaps the times we encountered a dark corner of our own souls that too easily found violent solutions for frustrating problems.

As we move through the Bible story from the womb of Eden to the resurrected beauty of the New Jerusalem, we experience all of life—the deserts and the oases—and the Bible reminds us that we are not alone on that adventure. The paths we take were well-traveled long before we arrived on this earth, and the stories shared by others have much to teach us about ourselves.

The people in the stories of Scripture want answers to the violence and suffering they have to endure, and some of them even openly wrestle with their own dark nature. They are us. The psalmist asks, "Why, O LORD, do you stand far off? Why do you hide yourself in times of trouble?," and we're right there asking the same thing. In response, the Bible tells us to stay awhile and listen. It has stories to tell about others who have suffered, others who have experienced loss, others who have committed violence, and what happened to them all.

A Better Question

"Why do bad things happen to good people?" is a question that assumes a textbook-style approach to Scripture. If we shift that question to the story approach, it becomes "Which Bible stories deal with suffering, and what can we learn from them?" Now *that* is a question the Bible is set to answer. As it turns out, suffering is a central theme in almost all of the biblical stories. The central narrative of the Old Testament is the Israelites' liberation from slavery, attained through the terrifying night of Passover, the creation of a covenant with God while the people quaked before a fiery mountain, and the people's discovery of a new form of faithfulness after destruction and exile. The central narrative for Christians is the story of a Rabbi who spends his life alleviating suffering and who is then arrested, mocked, tortured, and unjustly executed to achieve new life for all.

> "Why do bad things happen to good people?" is a question that assumes a textbook-style approach to Scripture. If we shift that question to the story approach, it becomes "Which Bible stories deal with suffering, and what can we learn from them?"

In both Testaments, grinding the lenses of faith with the stone of trial and persecution results in a clearer vision of God and a renewed commitment to bearing witness to that God in the world. In the Old Testament, it is framed as exile and return; in the New Testament, the themes are death and resurrection. But the witness of the biblical stories is that if you want the return and the resurrection, you must first endure exile and death. As with fearful passages, we're tempted to put aside the violent and suffering parts of Scripture. They don't feel good, and they bring things to the surface we would prefer to leave in the shadows. But, again, this is a story, and we don't understand the main point if we skip key parts of almost every chapter. Suffering in the Bible isn't an unfortunate sidebar; it's the necessary center. It's the purifying fire. Like Shadrach, Meshach, and Abednego in the fiery furnace . . . in we go.

Why Me? Sin, Suffering, and Friendly Fire

Apart from the story of Jesus, probably the best-known biblical story about suffering is the story of Job. There are two important things to understand before delving into the book of Job. The first is that "Job" rhymes with "robe," not "Bob." If you try to sound biblically literate by talking about someone having "the patience of Job" and pronounce it wrong, it won't go well. The second is that the book of Job, in its original Hebrew, begins with the linguistic equivalent of "Once upon a time." Job is not meant to be history, and there is zero evidence for the existence of a historical person who fits the description in the book that bears his name. It's a narrative folktale with a magnificent piece of epic poetry stuck in the middle.

If that strikes you as heresy, then go back and re-read the second chapter of this book. The beauty of stories is that they can be true without having to be factual. The story of poor Job is only free to show us truth about suffering when we can quit worrying that God is indifferent and cruel enough to make someone a pawn in a chess match with Satan. The bargain laid out at the beginning didn't literally happen. It's a literary device to frame the story and to present the issue that the story wants to address. And that issue is—you guessed it—suffering.

The story begins with God bragging about how pure and blameless Job is. Satan steps up to challenge that, claiming that Job is only living a good and holy life because he has it easy. Job has material wealth, a large, loving family, and good health. "Stretch out your hand now, and touch all that he has," says Satan, and that good boy will turn. "He will curse you to your face" (Job 1:11). The central question in the challenge is not "Why do good people suffer?" but rather "Why are good people good?" Do people worship God and live righteous lives only out of self-interest in a quid pro quo with God, or is there something deeper at play?

Satan may not be asking why bad things happen to good people, but Job certainly is. His worldview has always been that living a good life should warrant God's protection, if not from every bad turn of luck, at least from major harm. But now,

> *The central question in Satan's challenge is not "Why do good people suffer?" but rather "Why are good people good?"*

everything he values is torn away from him. He loses his wealth, then his family, and finally his health. It is clearly unfair, and Job is alternately deeply depressed and furious with God for allowing calamity after calamity when he has done nothing to deserve it. Job never curses God, but he does reach the point of cursing the day he was born. And then Job's "friends" come along and tell him it must be his fault.

The longer we live, the more we relate to Job. We've come to learn that we never get hit with just one thing; the bad news comes in waves. Like Job, we do our best to keep a stiff upper lip, but somewhere along the road of our lives we hit the superstorm that makes us just stop in our tracks and question everything we thought we knew about God, life, and the world around us. *Okay, I'm not perfect, but this, this I do not deserve. At. All.* By the time the prose narrative of Job switches to poetry, we're right there with

Job, upset at God and ready to land a holy left hook on any well-meaning friends who insist that we've brought it on ourselves.

That's what story does. It invites us into relationship with the characters so that we can experience life through them. In a story, we can explore from some distance what might happen if we find ourselves in a similar situation and respond as these characters do. If the Bible didn't contain stories of suffering and violence, we would gain no real benefit from it. Most of us respond well to moments of joy and good fortune. But all of us struggle to respond well when life's hammer thinks we're a nail. Stories let us explore the good times as well as the very bad times of others, helping us to withstand the dark days in our own lives.

Unlike story readers, the legal and textbook readers of Job are detached. Some have tossed the book because God seems callous and mean or because God never really answers the question about why innocent people suffer. Others are reading eagerly for the "answers," and are parsing the explanations for suffering offered by Job's friends. By the time they've read all of Job's trials and have seen that God not only restores but doubles Job's fortunes in the end, they have a very different takeaway than the story readers. As they see it, all we can know about suffering is that God is testing us for some inscrutable reason, and if we bear up while it's happening, God will give us twice as much as we had before.

A story-based view focuses on the experiences of life—all of them—and allows us to explore both the variety of experiences and the differing responses to them. The story reader is learning what kind of response eases suffering and what kind of response makes it worse. Except in the presentation of Jesus, the stories of the Bible don't intend to show us the perfect way to respond in any circumstance. Instead, they show us how people actually do respond in every circumstance imaginable. We see how faithful people respond, and we see how corrupt people respond. We see the complicated nature of the human soul, and, as we watch sinners become saints (or at least better people than they were before), we come to hold out more hope for the outcome of our own struggles.

A story-based view focuses on the experiences of life—all of them—and allows us to explore both the variety of experiences and the differing responses to them. The story reader is learning what kind of response eases suffering and what kind of response makes it worse.

The Bible as story gives us permission to be where we are and as we are, especially in our pain. It never implies that grief, rage, and all the things we feel when we suffer should be suppressed. There's a whole book of the Bible called Lamentations. And the chapters of that book are what the name implies: the wailing laments of those who have endured the unendurable. In the case of Lamentations, it is those who have lived through the horrors of war. In Job, it is the suffering of an individual, but the message is the same: There is nothing sinful or otherwise lacking in expressing our emotions when we suffer or in focusing on our own grief and pain.

When we enter the book of Job as a story, we feel not frustration, but relief. If we respond stoically when life beats us down, that's not wrong. If we cry out in anguish and question God's judgment and justice, that isn't a sin. If all we can manage to do is sit in the dust and scrape our own sores, we are in the company of the righteous who have suffered as we have. God doesn't condemn the honest response of those who suffer—not here in the book of Job nor anywhere else in the Bible. What God does condemn are Job's friends, who insist on making a legal case out of Job's story.

When Job's friends first come, they get it right. They enter Job's life and just sit with him in respectful silence. When we visit sites of great suffering—from the hospice bed of a loved one, to the death camp of Dachau, to the fields of terrible battles—we are usually met with silence. There's a reason graveyards and memorial monuments are quiet places. The book of Job suggests that while it's normal and acceptable to cry out and question in our suffering, there's no "answer" that doesn't somehow cheapen or minimize the anguish. To speak into the void of pain is yet another violation. To honor anguish, we can offer only presence, silent witness, and the loving balm that flows from heart to heart.

If you've ever done that with someone, however, you know it's exhausting, especially when it goes on for some time. That explains why there's a flurry of care and concern around the time of a funeral, but within several days the grieving find themselves lost in an empty house. And so it is with Job's friends. After a week of silence, they pull themselves out of Job's personal story and start providing "answers" to Job's dilemma. Now they're no longer sitting with him but passing judgment on him. Given his horrific circumstances, Job must have sinned, they insist. He must have done something to bring this on himself.

A legal approach to the book does exactly what the friends do. But if we've entered the story and are experiencing it along with Job, we know in our heart that the friends are dead wrong. The author told us at the beginning that Job is blameless. And we remember the times we ourselves have been hit hard by something out of the blue through no fault of our own. The story reader of Job knows what it feels like to have someone kick you when you're down and feels vindicated when God sums up the whole situation by directing Job's friends to ask for Job's forgiveness. Other stories in Scripture emphasize that sin causes suffering; but the story of Job helps us to remember that not all suffering is caused by sin.

Reading a story as story means we become a part of it. We accept the author's invitation to develop relationships with the characters and to imagine ourselves in their shoes. Immersing ourselves in the story of Job allows us to accept our emotions, which is critical in enduring the hurts and tragedies that life sends our way. It also helps us experience what it feels like when friends judge us. The story of Job teaches us what is *not* helpful when encountering the suffering of others. To know what the Bible thinks we *should* do, we need a different story.

Roadside Assistance:
The Parable of the Good Samaritan

We meet that different story in Luke, in the parable of the Good Samaritan. While the book of Job invites us to put ourselves in the shoes of someone in pain, the Good Samaritan story flips the perspective and asks us to imagine that we're perfectly fine but suddenly encounter suffering in someone else.

On its face, the parable is straightforward. A man is mugged and left for dead in the street. Through other lenses, we watch and see religious leaders—whom we would expect to care about a wounded person—pass by without so much as a kind word. We judge them, perhaps thinking of religious hypocrites that we may know. Then along comes a Samaritan, a person whom those first hearing the story would *never* expect to help—someone from a despised ethnic and religious group living just across Israel's border. And it is *that* person who, moved by compassion, treats the man's wounds, takes him to an inn, and pays for his care.

On its most basic level, the external, detached view isn't wrong. The Samaritan doesn't quiz the wounded man about why he was traveling alone on a dangerous road or ask to see his ID. There's no victim-blaming, and the story implies nothing about why the man was harmed, apart from the fact that robbers wanted his stuff. There's nothing like "So you must have sinned to have this happen to you. Will you confess?" or "Hey, if you wear expensive clothes, you're asking for it." While we know why Job suffered, we have no idea whether the mugged man was himself deeply flawed or pure as the driven snow. That's part of the point of the parable on its face: It doesn't matter. When confronted with suffering, you do what you can to help without asking if someone "deserves it" or not. When we pull the parable out of context and tell it, there's not much distortion.

But if we're moving along with the story, we've made a couple of stops before we get here that further the overall plot. Let's zoom out a bit to look at what prompted the parable. The stop just before this one shows us that the parable is told in response to a lawyer who would like a strict definition of who his "neighbor" is. The lawyer is squirming a bit because of the rather uncomfortable commandment in Leviticus 19:18 which says, "Love your neighbor as yourself." Jesus places great emphasis on that commandment, as does all of Judaism, so it's important to get it right. *But does my "neighbor" really mean ... uh ... that guy? So, how do you define "neighbor," exactly?* The man wants to know.

It's pretty typical for a lawyer to look at Scripture and see it as a legal text, but Jesus doesn't let this man do that. Instead of providing a legal definition of "neighbor" or going into a word study about the Leviticus passage, Jesus tells him—of course—a story. Once Jesus finishes the parable, he lets the man answer his own question. "Which of these three, do you think, was a neighbor to the man who fell into the hands of the robbers?" Jesus asks him. The lawyer doesn't miss a beat: "The one who showed him mercy." Once the law is presented as a story, the lawyer can leave his courtroom and enter into it. He can see himself walking down that road and know the answer to his question, even if he himself might be inclined to walk on by.

To really get the full impact of the parable, however, we need to zoom out one more stop and see the conversation between Jesus and the lawyer from the beginning. "Who is my neighbor?" is a follow-up question. The first question the lawyer poses is "What must I do to inherit eternal life?" Here, too, Jesus invites the man to answer his own question: "What is written in the law? What do you read there?" The lawyer knows his stuff, and he cites what any of his colleagues at the time would have answered: "You shall love the Lord your God with all your heart, and with all your soul, and with all your strength, and with all your mind; and your neighbor as yourself." Jesus commends him for his response. "You have given the right answer; do this, and you will live."

Viewing Scripture through a legal lens still allows this lawyer to produce an answer that is technically correct, but in other ways all wrong. His legal approach has taught him what the law *says*, but his desire to parse the word "neighbor" shows that he has never truly understood what the law *means*. He can recite it, but either he has no clue how to live it, or he wants a loophole to let him continue to live in a way that's most convenient for him. Law lets you do that. In story, however, the truth of God's law is learned through lived experience, and, once we're in it, the truth gets clearer page by page.

The technical answer to "What must I do to inherit eternal life?" is given in Scripture before the end of Deuteronomy: Love. Love God with all you've got and love your neighbor as yourself. The stories of God's people across the following millennia have invited us in to experience what happens when people try all the other options. Those stories landed their characters—and us with them—in wars, exile, and division. Jesus sums up the thousands of years of success and failure in a short parable about three responses to a wounded man. We put on the shoes of the priest, the Levite, and the Samaritan and walk that road from Jerusalem to Jericho. There's the man. Only we know whether we would have stopped to help or walked on by, but from within the story we know which response is God's preference. The response God wants is compassion—to witness to God's love by showing it in action.

From "Why?" to "What If?"

The Bible doesn't give us a nice, neat answer to "Why do bad things happen to good people?" In fact, it doesn't usually answer any kind of question that starts with "Why?," even though the Bible itself is full of people asking exactly that. More typically, the stories of the Bible seek to turn our "Why" questions into "What if" questions. When dealing with the subject of suffering, we are led to questions like "What if something awful happens to me? What should I do?" or "What if I encounter suffering in someone else? How should I respond?"

Other lenses for reading Scripture detach us from the suffering we observe. As a result, when we test those answers in the fires of life, they quickly turn to ash. They have no real substance underneath. In order to understand not just what the Bible says but what it means, we need the invitation of story to inhabit the characters and see the world through their eyes. When we enter a story and see not "them" but ourselves, we come away with fewer "answers" but more substance. We are left not with ash, but with gold. And, like the three men in Daniel who are joined by "a god" in the fiery furnace, we are amazed to find that God is walking in our midst.

CHAPTER 7

The Unseen

....

Encountering Mystery and Miracle

There are more things in heaven and earth, Horatio,
Than are dreamt of in your philosophy.

—Hamlet, Act I, scene 5

While the issue most troubling to Bible readers is God's
seeming complicity in suffering, running a close second is
the issue surrounding the miracles and other supernatural
elements in the Bible. To me, the more curious matter is
why anyone would expect that a collection of texts whose
central character is God *wouldn't* include the supernatural, but the issue still causes many people to cut certain
chapters out of the story. By now we should realize that
playing Thomas Jefferson by cutting out all the parts of
the Bible we don't like blows up our car and keeps us from
reaching our destination. Story needs to follow the road all

the way in order to make any sense; so let's pull over, clean the windshield, and examine our eyewear.

When we look at the Bible with law or science lenses, entire sections get blurred beyond recognition. Looking at stories of the supernatural while wearing science lenses makes the stories seem stupid, funny, or quaint reminders of a more ignorant age. But when we put on the story lenses, those other-worldly things come into focus. Just as the supernatural element is beyond human experience, so the story that contains such an element is pointing to something beyond itself. It's a sign.

Signs, Signs, Everywhere Are Signs

Miracles in the Bible are not God showing off superpowers; they are signs. In the Gospel of John, the word "miracle" doesn't even appear. The events that the other Gospels call "miracles," John calls "signs." Those miraculous events aren't just for ratings. They have a purpose, and that purpose is to signify that the person doing them is speaking or acting with God's authority.

We see Jesus performing miraculous healings, even to the point of raising the dead, and we associate these with acts of compassion. There's no doubt that Jesus felt compassion for those he healed, but there were hundreds if not thousands of sick people—not to mention legions of dead people—that Jesus did nothing at all about. Either Jesus was very selective about his compassion, or he was doing something else entirely. John's Gospel suggests it was the latter. When Jesus performed a miracle, it was either a sign of his divine authority or a clue about the nature of his overall mission. The miracles in the Bible serve the purpose of giving authority and legitimacy to the person performing them and/or signaling the larger purpose of the endeavor.

Miracles in the Bible are not God showing off super-powers; they are signs. In the Gospel of John, the word "miracle" doesn't even appear. The events that the other Gospels call "miracles," John calls "signs."

Now remember the ability of stories to form relationships and shape identity and think about the reasons for compiling an entire book of stories that detail the religious history of a people. It wouldn't be unreasonable to expect history to be dotted with signs that Jews and Christians found meaningful: signs that their God could beat the pants off of other gods, signs that their heroes had God's wind at their backs, signs that the justice and peace promised by their prophets would one day come to pass, signs that death would not have the last word.

If miracles are signs, then they don't have to be supernatural to serve their purpose. Too much ink has been spilled by people trying to "disprove" a miracle by showing that there's a perfectly earthly explanation for what happened: a comet for the star of Bethlehem; a confusion of the shallow Reed Sea with the much deeper Red Sea; a mutual sharing of food instead of a miraculous multiplication of loaves and fishes. Like "truth" and "facts," "miracle" and "supernatural" have become equated. So, if someone can prove that Jesus just knew where the rocks were, then his walking on water is disproven as a miracle, he is shown to be a fraud, the Bible isn't true, and there is no God. Or so they claim. It's a pointless and divisive exercise. And yet, for detached readers looking for fact-based truth, it's almost impossible for them not to get caught up in that argument.

But those of us who take a story-based view are too busy experiencing the miracle from within to ask those questions. As we join the frightened disciples in the boat, watching Jesus walk to us on the water, our response is instinctive. We don't lean back and say, "Hey, people can't walk on water. What's the trick?" Instead, we say, "Whoa! Who is this guy?" Without any textual analysis at all, we know that we're seeing a sign about the identity and authority of Jesus. And that's exactly what happens with the disciples in that story. Their takeaway is summed up in Matthew 14:33: "Truly you are the Son of God."

When we experience truly amazing things in the context of our daily lives, we don't analyze them as "natural" or "supernatural." They're simply remarkable things happening to us, and we respond in awe. The appearance of a rainbow across a dreary sky can come to us as a miracle, despite what we know about the spectrum of light, weather, and all the science that accounts for a rainbow forming at the end of a storm. We know all about conception and birth, yet every newborn comes to us as pure miracle. Miracles aren't necessarily supernatural. They're unexpected signs that make us stop and wonder if we really know as much as we think we do and question whether there's a deeper meaning to this life that we have yet to explore. Our awareness of a natural explanation doesn't change the sign.

But what if signs are supernatural? Is that possible? If we're considering the inspiration of Scripture through legal or scientific lenses, the answer to that question matters a lot. The truth to which the sign points must have an objective reality when we look through those glasses. But what happens when we look at those signs as part of a larger story? We always look for signs when we're reading a story, whether it's noticing that Madame Defarge knits at interesting times or that a dog didn't bark. Back in Chapter 5, we saw how that works in the Bible with snake signs. Asking if there's a natural explanation for an event that's presented as supernatural is a question that the story lens can't even see, let alone answer. The better question for our lens is "What does this event signify to those who experienced it?" And, if we've accepted story's invitation to join the characters on the page, we probably won't have to ask that question at all. We'll know, because we're there.

As readers of the entire story of the Bible, we're given an advantage that none of the individual biblical characters have. They see and experience only the signs of their particular lives and circumstances. We get to see them all. And, by the time we've entered the stories of God's people across several millennia, we're in a position to see patterns on a large scale.

While each individual miracle or divine appearance may be a sign particular to that story or person, the continuous flow of angels, miraculous occurrences, and other kinds of supernatural events becomes a more general sign of something much greater. Perhaps, when taken together, the supernatural events and beings of the Bible signify that the world is far more complex and exists in many more dimensions than we mortals understand. Some of us are more comfortable with that possibility than others.

Behold, I Show You a Mystery

Mystery novels have an ardent following. If you're one of those readers, you know that a cardinal sin of reading a mystery novel is turning to the last page first—to get the answer to *whodunit* without having first gone through the winding plot and pages of clever clues that take you there. But this transgression pales in comparison to the sin of a mystery writer who takes you to that last page and then says, "Sorry, it's unsolvable. There's no way to tell who did it." Such a writer would have to enter the federal witness-protection program.

We like the thrill of a good mystery, but we very much want it solved—if not by our own cunning, then at least by those charged with making sure everything is stable and secure and all wrapped up as it should be. In the end, we want to know. The mystery doesn't have to be a crime in a novel. We may simply want to know how something works, or what would happen if we combined this thing with that thing, or what lies just around the corner. The mystery feels good and exciting to us specifically because we plan to turn that mystery into knowledge. We plan to find out who or what or where or why. This explains why we can become annoyed when Bible stories toss in unexplained things that are beyond our mystery-book expectations.

Our relationship to mystery is complicated. We don't just hate it, or there would be no audience for mystery novels or for almost any drama put to page or film. Mystery itself is exciting and can make us happy. In fact, psychologists tell us that when we take a vacation, we feel the happiest before we go—during the time that we look forward to it. We're happier then than we are during the time we're away, even if we go to exotic locales and have a wonderful time. We're happier anticipating the experience, the mystery of it, than actually having the experience itself.

It's that way with other types of mystery, too. Solving the mystery can be anticlimactic in a way. If and when we go back to the book, the once-mysterious device, the island without the fog that used to shroud its secrets, the first excitement of possibility is replaced with the comfort of the known. Both are good things, but they're different things, and accomplishing the latter eliminates the former.

To keep our balance, we need both in our lives. Some amount of mystery is fun and exciting. But we don't want everything to be a mystery, which is why major life changes, like going off to college or moving to a new part of the country, are so stressful. We don't want to lose all our old friends and familiar haunts. We need to rest in the comfort of familiar things if we're to muster the courage to explore something new.

Each of us has a certain level of tolerance for the unknown. Some are happy with a lot, some with just a little. Some are adamant that mysteries must be resolved promptly, while others are content to leave questions unanswered for another day or week or even indefinitely. Some delight in shrouding themselves with mystery; others prefer to be an open book. Some love surprises; others will write you out of their will if you throw them a surprise party. And all those personalities are exposed and sometimes come into conflict when it comes to the *magnum mysterium* of faith and spirituality.

Trying to prove or disprove a miracle or supernatural event in the Bible changes nothing and, in many instances, doesn't really matter to the overall "truth" of the story. That said, while you might think of wandering into a Christian church and saying that it doesn't matter if Jesus literally rose from the dead, I wouldn't recommend it.

The battle royal over miracles in the Bible is waged over the central miracle of the New Testament: the resurrection of Jesus. Since the moment of the event forward, arguments about it have raged. Can the central, miraculous event of the New Testament—the event that underlies all of Christian faith—be trusted?

Proving Jesus's resurrection is both like and unlike proving the existence of God. On the one hand, there is no serious scholar who doubts the physical existence of Jesus, born in roughly the same time and place and dying in a way that is consistent with the outline presented to us in the Bible. So, unlike the existence of God, the existence of a first-century Jewish man named Jesus who was raised in Nazareth and was crucified by the Romans has been proven at least beyond a reasonable doubt. The person who tells you otherwise is not wearing either textbook or story glasses; they're wearing fake-news glasses. There is consensus both inside and outside the church that Jesus existed.

The battle royal over miracles in the Bible is waged over the central miracle of the New Testament: the resurrection of Jesus. Since the moment of the event forward, arguments about it have raged. Can the central, miraculous event of the New Testament—the event that underlies all of Christian faith—be trusted?

The Resurrection, however, is another matter. The event itself is not described in the Bible. In all four versions of the story, the women come to the tomb on Easter morning and find it empty. And, even within the pages of Scripture itself, the conspiracy theories about what happened have already started. The Gospel of Matthew tells us that the guards at the tomb were bribed by the priests and elders to tell people that Jesus's disciples came and stole the body. But it's clear that at least the story of Jesus, including all the stories about him that follow in the rest of the New Testament, is built on the belief that Jesus physically and literally rose from the dead. Jesus makes appearances to his disciples and others with enough physical presence that Thomas can touch the wounds in his hands and sides.

But, apart from the claims of the stories, did it happen? Did Jesus physically rise from the dead? Like the existence of God, it can't be either proven or disproven from this distance in time with the tools that we have. We either believe the accounts are factual or we don't. We either take it on faith or we don't. The lens of story adds nothing to the question, because story is not the lens we use when we're looking for facts.

Looking through the lens of story can't tell us if something actually happened or not. It doesn't even tell us if the answer to that question matters or not. The lens of story completely blurs out the answers to both of those questions. What our story glasses can show us is that the Resurrection happened *in the story* and that accepting this plot twist matters to understanding the story as a whole. And, when the story is a miracle like rising from the dead, the lens of story shows us a sign to mark that moment as critically important to understanding everything that follows.

The insistence that mysteries must be solved in an empirical way isn't only a problem for those who want natural explanations for supernatural events. When it comes to biblical interpretation, Christians generally have been ill-served by those who want their mysteries laid bare and dissected. Early church councils couldn't just say, "Well, the doctrine of the Trinity is a mystery that we live into." They had to spend time trying to solve the mystery—to know what is ultimately unknowable. It allowed for the identification of a lot of heretics, but not much else. And it certainly didn't end up making it any easier to explain the Trinity to a congregation on a Sunday morning. Ditto for the exact nature of Holy Communion, and a lot of other doctrines and rituals of the church.

It's no different when it comes to Jesus's death and resurrection. We Christians can't manage simply to recognize it and honor it as a sign of God's work among us. We feel the need to dissect it and explain in great detail just how that series of events saved the world. And we're in good company. Many of the personalities in the New Testament try to do the same thing. But maybe that esteemed company with their diversity of views is also part of our very human story of having no tolerance for living with mystery and fighting even our closest allies if we can't settle on one correct "answer."

Accepting the supernatural parts of the Bible as something ultimately unknowable—whether it's the miracles or the angels, demons, and other creatures in the spiritual realms—feels a lot like leaving home. The world we thought we knew turns strange. But that very strangeness is a sign that there is much yet to learn. There are more things in heaven and earth than are dreamt of in our philosophy, and the lens of story will point us to them.

The story lens doesn't invite us into a new world. It invites us into a new way of seeing our current world. If I look at my chair, I see a solid, sturdy piece of furniture. But if I look at that same chair through a powerful microscope, I'll see a sea of vibrating particles. Once I stop looking through the microscope, the chair will still be there, looking just as solid and stationary as it did before. What happened? The microscope didn't transport me into a fictional world. It allowed me to see a truth about the chair that I couldn't see with the naked eye. The chair was just as real with the lens of the microscope as it was with my natural eyes. But I now understand something new about it because for a moment I used a different lens to see it. Seeing the Bible as story is not a way of ignoring facts or of verifying them. It's a lens for seeing a different kind of truth about the world.

Ignorance Is Bliss

Part of that different truth is learning to see a spiritual dimension to life and to recognize signs that point us in more helpful directions. We gain the courage to open that spiritual door from the story's overarching promise that a loving God goes with us and that it turns out well in the end. When all is said and done, the mystery will be resolved. But the Bible doesn't put up with the human arrogance of our thinking we know all there is to know in the here and now. To live in community with others, we need humility. It's a key biblical virtue. And there's nothing that will produce humility quite so much as an angel with a big sword blocking your path and explaining that you're even more stupid than your talking donkey. Miracles do have a secondary function.

The point here isn't whether the story of Balaam and his loquacious ass happened exactly the way Numbers 22 describes. Our story glasses make that issue irrelevant. But the lens of story does *not* filter out the larger message that until we admit our own fundamental ignorance, we will be incapable of learning or accomplishing anything of significance. We may not proceed; we may not pass biblical Go and collect 200 drachmas until we can admit that, when it comes right down to it, we don't know squat.

Historian and author Dr. Yuval Noah Harari claims,

"The Scientific Revolution has not been a revolution of knowledge. It has been above all a revolution of ignorance. The great discovery that launched the Scientific Revolution was the discovery that humans do not know the answers to their most important questions." That makes sense. Harari's point is not just that we have gaps in our knowledge, but that we are ignorant of the answers to life's most significant questions. The Scientific Revolution wasn't just about realizing that things could be better with new discoveries. It was about realizing that we were so fundamentally ignorant that we were, as a species, in jeopardy.

The Bible concurs with this assessment, making it pretty clear that we humans are not the brightest bulbs and usually have trouble getting out of our own way. The repeated biblical metaphor comparing humans to sheep is not a compliment. I've owned sheep and can say this with confidence. In Matthew, Jesus compares the guidance of the religious leaders to "blind guides of the blind." When Peter can't figure out what Jesus means by that, Jesus responds, "Are you still so dull?"

Isaiah quotes God as saying, "For my thoughts are not your thoughts, nor are your ways my ways, says the Lord." In the Bible, human beings are qualitatively different beings than God. We are made in God's image and are able to serve as vessels for God's spirit; but, ultimately,

God is God and we're not. We are limited. We can see, but not clearly. We can have thoughts, but we are free to choose courses of action that are not God's way, often with serious consequence.

If you remember, that inability to accept our own ignorance is what got us into trouble in the first place, at least according to Genesis. Human beings ate from the tree of the knowledge of good and evil. The verb for "knowing" in Hebrew (the original language of Genesis) is experiential, not intellectual. Adam "knew" Eve, and they conceived a child. That didn't happen because they read a book on making babies. Eve's reaching out for the fruit of that tree wasn't just saying that she and Adam wanted

> The verb for "knowing" in Hebrew (the original language of Genesis) is experiential, not intellectual.

to understand the nature of good and evil as an intellectual exercise. They wanted to "know" them in the biblical sense, to experience both things and thereby come to full knowledge. They wanted to literally conceive good and evil, even though God had warned them that death would be a certain consequence. The very first warning in the Bible is that there are some roads we shouldn't take, some fruit we shouldn't eat. Not because our doing so threatens God, but because it threatens us.

The stories of the Bible don't seek to stifle knowledge;

they seek to direct our learning toward the ways of God. They encourage us to seek to know good but not evil, to discover ways to further acts of compassion, care, and community rather than destruction, death, and division.

An Answer in Search of a Question

We are understandably anxious about living with unanswered questions. If our questions are important, then so are the ways we answer them. But when it comes to the Bible (and religion more generally), there really are very few "answers." There are a variety of opinions, some more grounded in scholarship than others, but obvious "answers" to which everyone assents are hard to come by. The entire realm of religion—its truth claims, its sacred texts, its doctrines and dogmas—all of it operates mostly outside of the realm of fact. That means its questions also operate primarily outside of the realm of "answers."

The entire realm of religion—its truth claims, its sacred texts, its doctrines and dogmas—all of it operates mostly outside of the realm of fact. That means its questions also operate primarily outside of the realm of "answers."

While the story lens fixes some of that, we're often resistant to wearing those lenses because uncertainty about basic facts is unsettling. We're afraid that if we take off the glasses we're used to, we'll fall into a ditch. But what story lenses reveal is that if we're wearing our legal or scientific glasses while looking at the Bible, we're actually in the ditch already. All we can do with those old glasses is dig the hole deeper. With the lens of story, we can spot the stairs that bring us out of the ditch and up where we can see the entire vista before us.

What that vista reveals is that the thing most important to story is not answers, but questions. It is questions that keep us turning the page, moving forward not just with a novel but with our lives. The Quakers have a wonderful tradition called the Clearness Committee. When someone is stuck, they can ask other members to form a Clearness Committee to help them come to clarity about what to do. The brilliant part is that the Clearness Committee doesn't make a decision for the person who's stuck.

Instead of giving advice or direction, they listen to the questions of the struggling person and help make them better questions. Clearness about what to do comes not from an outside opinion, biblical or otherwise. It comes from the person in the dilemma arriving at the best question for a situation. When you know what question to ask, your direction becomes clear. Not easy, maybe, but clear.

We often assume that God has all the answers, and,

since we believe God is good, we have trouble thinking that God would leave us hanging without the answers we seek. It seems reasonable to us that God would put all those answers into the Bible, even if they might be in some sort of code that different epochs of time and place need to decipher. But that's not how it works. Which is not to say that the Bible isn't God-breathed or holy or helpful or *truthful*. It is to say, in yet another way, that truth and facts are different things.

An answer book simply isn't what God gave us, coded or otherwise, because we don't build relationships through textbooks or legal codes. Instead, God gave us stories and questions for us to reflect on together. The most exciting Bible studies I've participated in haven't been those when I've taken questions to the Bible and found answers. They've been when I've taken questions to the Bible and come away with *even better* questions, and the discussions about them have kept me exploring with others long into the night.

CHAPTER 8

20/20 Vision

Stories That Bear Fruit

There are those that look at things the way they are, and ask why? I dream of things that never were, and ask why not?

—Robert F. Kennedy

Back when the first homo sapiens were banging out hand axes with rocks, something happened. In his brilliant book about human history, *Sapiens*, Yuval Noah Harari calls it the "Cognitive Revolution," and he means the point in human history where homo sapiens went beyond being able only to describe what *was* and started telling stories about what *might be*. In short, they developed fiction—the imaginative capacity to conceive of things beyond their own experience and understanding. After the Cognitive Revolution, humans could ask not only "What?" but "What if?"

Harari, a history professor at Hebrew University in Jerusalem, claims it was this new ability that propelled homo sapiens to dominance across the earth. With their newfound imagination, our earliest ancestors could devise multiple scenarios for their daily lives, whether or not such things had ever happened before. They could conceive not only of gods, but of religious identity and practice. With this new ability, they could develop laws to mobilize people into abstract collective bodies like corporations and nations. The Cognitive Revolution allowed huge numbers of people to unite, not just because of common biology, but for common purpose—a vision of a possible future, imagined by individuals and transmitted through stories of what might be if we could work toward it together.

Imagine

The stories of the Bible couldn't have existed before the Cognitive Revolution, because they describe and advocate for future possibility. Hope has no meaning apart from an imagined future. The very idea of a "Promised Land," either somewhere on the physical earth or in a life beyond, wouldn't have been possible without that shift. Neither would the structure of religious identity and prac-

tice that we see as early as the moral struggle in Adam and
Eve when they heard God's command not to eat from a
certain tree, and the offering presented to God by Cain
and Abel. The Bible contains some of the earliest descrip-
tions of what life looked like when homo sapiens put on
their first pair of story glasses.

The stories of the Bible don't just describe a world; they
give meaning to it and shape a worldview with a purposeful
beginning, middle, and end. We hear of an earth created out
of chaos by a God of order; human activity straining with
the tensions between cor-
ruption and virtue; a people
taking two steps forward
and one step back, inching
forward in fits and starts
toward an ultimate era of
justice and peace; and all of
it directed by the hand of a

> *The stories of the Bible don't just describe a world; they give meaning to it and shape a worldview with a purposeful beginning, middle, and end.*

loving God. The events of history are woven with interpre-
tations of the past and hopes for the future to create a complex and multilayered meta-story of a particular people who
worshiped a particular God.

The broad arc of the biblical narrative speaks to the
near-universal desire for some version of that "promised
land," a place of abundance and peace that might come
to exist either in this world or another. But the Bible goes

beyond just casting a utopian vision. It also outlines specific ways that people of all ages can work together toward that goal, giving us the potential to transcend our smaller identities and to see ourselves as part of a much larger, unified body. The Bible is also clear that reaching such a potential is not without its challenges and setbacks, even for those who want it most.

The tensions between staying with a smaller, biological identity and merging to form a more universal body are evident in many places in both testaments. The overall story and its vision of unity comes to us in disconnected pieces, much like human history itself, because the stories of the Bible are not from any one age. But those pieces are threaded together with the tensile promise that no exile is forever, and no darkened depth is beneath the reach of God's guiding light. The stories recognize the exile and the dark, often by showing them in brutal detail. But the thread of hope is always picked up again, a swinging firepot showing the way through the gloom.

The world-altering consequences of the Cognitive Revolution show the power of story. Stories are literally how human beings have been able to organize and collaborate to bring us to the modern era. And, as I write this in the summer of 2017, it's the battle over stories—the competing narratives about the very fabric of human identity, nature, and purpose—that will determine whether we will move toward a new phase of cooperation or into a final stage of annihilation. The stories we choose to guide our lives matter, now more than ever.

But how are we to access the stories of the Bible in a way that leads to cooperation and not annihilation? The Bible has a pretty checkered past in that regard. Using the lens of story is certainly helpful, but the Bible is still no easy lift. In fact, many see the Bible as simply too toxic, a corrupting influence that needs to be silenced if the world is ever to know peace. And they have a point. There's ample evidence of the Bible being weaponized for destruction on both an individual and a worldwide scale.

Are the Bible's detractors correct in their assessment? Christians shouldn't just point fingers and cry foul. That attitude on the part of the Bible's defenders is part of the reason its stories fall prey to destructive use in the first place. We must always ask if the critics are right and consider the evidence they present. What is it that makes a story toxic, and does the Bible—either as a whole or in part—fit that description?

Toxic Stories

Stories don't exist in a vacuum. The story is the means by which a relationship is created between a storyteller and an audience, and the attitudes and life experience of both sides help to determine the power and the effects of the story. That means that if you encounter a toxic story, it might be hard to tell whether the story started out as toxic or whether a toxic substance was injected into a once-helpful narrative by the storyteller.

One way to sort that out is to examine the history of a given story. If a story is toxic in and of itself, it will always have a toxic effect. That's what toxins do—they're poison. You might be poisoned a little or a lot, but if you ingest a poison, at least some part of you will be harmed. Toxic stories always do harm to everything they touch, including the storytellers.

An example of a toxic story is the story of white supremacy, which has always led to division, hatred, anger, and death. I can think of no instance where a group or nation became a safer or happier place when that story was allowed to flourish. In America, it almost immediately corrupted the otherwise courageous story of pilgrims searching for religious freedom. My *Mayflower* ancestors came to believe they were superior to the Native Peoples they found here. Exile and genocide followed. That dark behavior was followed by the abduction of Africans to sell as slaves to white "masters." Slavery inflicted humiliation, torture, and death on the slaves and to this day is a stain on the stories of many of America's founders and leading lights. The faith of white Christians who adopted that story was corrupted, and it tainted their witness.

The toxic story of white supremacy did not abate, leading to the Civil War. It took the lives of 620,000 soldiers, and hateful embers still flare up over 150 years later. Even the joyous story of emancipation bears the stench of the poisonous supremacy story that warped it into Jim Crow and that continues to soil every advance in race relations through voter suppression, intimidation, and hate crimes spilling blood into today's news. White supremacy is an irredeemable, toxic story—no matter who tells it. The story of white supremacy kills those who hear it and rots the souls of those who tell it.

I wanted to use this toxic story specifically, because one of the things white supremacy has poisoned is the Bible. White supremacist Christians took it up and warped it to tell white supremacy stories. As a result, their faith was poisoned. Those who heard it, white and black alike, were injected with toxins, and the Bible itself was stained with their hate. And that abominable use of the Bible hasn't stopped.

And yet, history shows us that the opposite has also been true, even in that same racial struggle. Other storytellers took that same Bible in those same situations and instead lifted up the story of God freeing the Hebrew slaves from their bondage in Egypt. There's a reason that abolitionist Harriet Tubman became known as "Moses." It's not an accident that the leader of the civil rights movement in America was a Christian minister, or that the dream preached by the Rev. Dr. Martin Luther King Jr. came straight out of the Bible's promise of freedom and justice. In another setting, it was the stories of the Bible that led Mother Teresa out into the streets of Calcutta to care for "the least of these." Are those the signs of a fundamentally toxic story?

In the case of white supremacy, the stories themselves are toxic. Truly toxic things can only corrupt. But the stories of the Bible have been used to foster some of the greatest good the world has ever seen, a feat that would be impossible if their essential nature was toxic. The stories of the Bible become corrupted by external forces, not internal ones—by storytellers who either knowingly or unknowingly bring an outside poison to their retelling or who lift a story of harm out of its context, cutting the threads of hope that connect oppressive texts to the larger biblical vision of a better way.

When we see the Bible as essentially story, it allows us to include the nature of the storyteller into our evaluation of its message. That includes the way the story is being transmitted to us in the moment as well as the way the story may have been presented to us in the past. It also includes the particular people who first recorded the stories and the various reasons they had for telling them the way they did. When encountering the Bible, it's important to ask if we're really judging the story itself, or if the message we're receiving might be distorted by a confused or corrupted storyteller.

We also should evaluate whether we ourselves, as the ones who receive the story, are bringing any kind of contamination with us. We might not be bringing white supremacy, but are we bringing Western supremacy or a belief that the modern age is morally superior to earlier times? Are we Christians bringing Christian supremacy to Jewish texts? Are we bringing a twenty-first-century expectation to an Early Stone Age text? More directly to the point of this book, are we bringing the right set of glasses? Does a story become toxic because we're seeing it through a legal or scientific lens? Are we taking a metaphor literally or confusing truth and facts?

The Bible is not without its challenging and confusing stories, especially when left to stand on their own. Unfortunately, that is the way most people encounter them. A fifteen-minute sermon on a Sunday morning may not even give us more than a few verses, let alone a whole story. And because the power of a story is activated only when it is both told and received, it's relatively easy for any story to be warped by those who mix their own agendas with the telling. How do we know that a charismatic storyteller isn't leading us down a dark and noxious path? How do we keep the story out of polluted waters? And, even more importantly, how do we keep from polluting it ourselves? It's complicated.

The Myth of Simplicity

The Bible is a complicated collection of texts on many levels, which would be just fine if human beings automatically gravitated toward complex and nuanced things. But we don't. We want our information in 140 characters or less. The Bible has now been translated into emojis. We want our Bible simple and quick in easy-to-understand sound bites, just like we want everything else.

Part of that is an understandable reaction to how complicated everything has gotten—even things that used to seem simple. Once upon a time you could walk into a store, buy a loaf of bread, and not give it a second thought. Now we're taught that our health and the health of anyone who eats at our table is at risk if we don't buy that bread wisely. We must walk into a grocery store and face a full wall of varieties of bread and then read and understand lists of ingredients and nutrition labels—some of which are actually designed to be misleading. And, if we haven't done our homework ahead of time, we don't even know what we're looking for on those labels. We long for simpler times.

But the reality is that bread has always been complicated. It was easy for us as consumers only because we had placed our trust in the companies that made the bread and the retail stores that sold it to us. When large conglomerates were exposed as caring more for their bottom line than the health of their customers, that trust was broken, and the complexities of deciding what was healthy landed in the lap of the consumer. The notion that some things used to be simple is false. Some things used to be simple only because we trusted others to sort through the complexity for us, whether it was the grocer or the priest.

In twenty-first-century America, we're overwhelmed with complexity in part because we trust no one. We don't trust the government, we don't trust the media, we don't trust the church, we don't trust the schools, we don't trust the corporations, we don't really trust our neighbors, and sometimes we even look over our shoulders at family members. We only trust ourselves, and every time we click on a link with a computer virus or fall for an e-mail scam, we're not even sure we can do that.

Human beings like a challenge, but we don't want everything to be a challenge, and the more important the thing is to our lives, the easier we want it to be. So it's understandable that when we hear that the Bible—the book supposedly holding the information about the salvation of our souls—is complex, we get testy. We're left with two basic options. We can try to learn everything about everything and attempt to sort through the complexities ourselves, or we can try to re-establish trust once again. After all, the problem isn't that no one is trustworthy; the problem is that we no longer know how to identify trustworthy people, organizations, and institutions.

Human beings like a challenge, but we don't want everything to be a challenge, and the more important the thing is to our lives, the easier we want it to be. So it's understandable that when we hear that the Bible—the book supposedly holding the information about the salvation of our souls—is complex, we get testy.

It might seem like learning to identify those who are trustworthy is yet another complicated process for which we have little energy. But Jesus taught us to make that discernment—we've talked about it before: "You will know them by their fruits." Once we started picking up lovely red tomatoes in the Acme Grocery Store and found they tasted like chilled cardboard, we knew something was up. The sign said "fresh," but we knew better when we tasted them. Eventually we learned to trust a given grocery store because the taste of their fruit confirmed the claim of "fresh, ripe tomatoes" on their sign. If it's a biblical story we're evaluating, then it's biblical fruit we're looking for, both in the storytellers and in the communities who try to live out the story as they understand it.

Fruitful Stories

On an individual level, Paul calls those qualities the "fruit of the Spirit": love, joy, peace, patience, kindness, generosity, faithfulness, gentleness, and self-control. When those who are telling the Christian story don't show evidence of that fruit, it's time to look for another tree. They can't be trusted to tell the stories properly because the fruit of their lives shows they've never understood them or taken them seriously in the first place. In some cases a person is simply too new to the story to tell it effectively. Many fruit trees take several seasons to produce any fruit. There's a reason that the best storytellers are often ripe with age.

But the spiritual qualities of the storyteller are just one measure of the story's fruit. Another is whether living out a particular story produces a result that looks more like heaven and less like hell. Even if we've decided we can trust the storyteller, we need to ask if the story itself is trustworthy. What sort of fruit does it produce in the community as a whole? Does an attempt to live the story move us toward the Bible's ultimate vision? Does it seem like we're headed in the right direction? To evaluate that, we have to see that vision clearly for ourselves.

Apart from the initial paradise in the Garden of Eden, arguably the two most famous scenes of "heaven" in the Bible are from Isaiah 11–12 and Revelation 21–22. On the surface, the settings of the two are quite different. In Isaiah, the scene is pastoral. The wolf and the lamb, the leopard and the goat, the calf and the lion are all getting along famously. The carnivores have reverted to a vegetarian diet (which is how it was in Genesis until after the Great Flood), and little children are playing near venomous snakes without threat of harm. "They will not hurt or destroy on all my holy mountain," God says in Isaiah 11:9. We have come to call that vision "The Peaceable Kingdom," after the title of a series of sixty-two paintings based on the scene by American Quaker Edward Hicks.

In the Revelation passages the setting is quite different. There we have not a pasture, but a city, the New Jerusalem, with a lot of ink spent on the rare jewels and precious substances that comprise its gates, foundation, and walls. Why do we think of heaven as having streets of gold? "And the twelve gates are twelve pearls, each of the gates is a single pearl, and the street of the city is pure gold, transparent as glass." And there's no need to argue about coal or solar power. "The city has no need of sun or moon to shine on it, for the glory of God is its light, and its lamp is the Lamb."

On every Palm Sunday of my childhood, this vision rang from our church sanctuary as the choir sang "The Holy City," written in 1892 by Michael Maybrick and Frederic Weatherly. Its power was well-known. A story recorded in the *African Methodist Episcopal Church Review* in 1911 describes an opera singer awaiting trial in a jail cell while a judge in an adjacent courtroom went through his caseload. From his cell, the opera singer began to sing "The Holy City," the lyrics of which move from describing the old Jerusalem, through the darkness of the cross, and ultimately to the vision of the promised New Jerusalem: "The light of God was on its streets, the gates were open wide, and all who would might enter, and no one was denied."

As the story goes, all within the courtroom heard the song and, as it progressed, began to weep and fall to their knees. By the end of the song, the judge saw the humanity in every defendant before him and, with one kind word, dismissed them all without so much as a fine. Now that's an example of a vision producing the fruit that it promises. Whether the utopian vision will one day exist as it is described is something we can't know. But watching the effect of the vision when the story is told tells us whether it's more likely to heal the nations or set them on a path to war.

"They will not hurt or destroy on all my holy mountain."

A community we can trust not only talks about that kind of vision but shows glimpses of that vision becoming reality in their midst. They seek to live the story and produce the fruit.

> A trustworthy community, in terms of its biblical faithfulness, works every minute of every day to have less hurt and destruction in the world, starting with its own members. Stories are seeds planted in our hearts and minds. We learn whether they are healing stories or toxic stories by observing the fruit of those who tell them and the fruit of the communities who seek to live by them.

A trustworthy community, in terms of its biblical faithfulness, works every minute of every day to have less hurt and destruction in the world, starting with its own members. Stories are seeds planted in our hearts and minds. We learn whether they are healing stories or toxic stories by observing the fruit of those who tell them and the fruit of the communities who seek to live by them.

There's no magical way to approach the Bible that will prevent its use in harmful ways. But when we see the Bible as story, it can lessen those misunderstandings and give us a better foundation for creating the kind of loving and just community the Bible envisions.

I See You

This book began with an exploration of story as the most basic building block of human relationships. Stories are how we come to understand ourselves, each other, and our purpose in the world. The stories we allow into our lives and the ways in which we share those stories with others matter profoundly because sharing those stories determines how or even if we see one another.

If we see the Bible as law, sharing its contents with each other places us in a courtroom, judge and jury at the ready, with a tense and adversarial view of Scripture that the text itself does not share. Someone somewhere is in the dock when we take our biblical legal team out to interrogate them. Likewise, if we see the Bible as a collection of answers and facts, we're seated in a classroom, anxious about exams and struggling—even sometimes cheating—in order to know the answers and be found acceptable. Those lenses leave us nervous and prone to struggle in a competitive environment.

But if we see the Bible as story, we can see ourselves gathered around a campfire or getting together for a meal. We relax and easily allow our imaginations to inhabit those characters from long ago to experience the events as they did. Even if the circumstances are devastating, telling and sharing these stories is a way to acknowledge that we're in this together—we're here for each other. With story we can recognize that those communities and characters from long ago are somehow our people, too. We may be huddled in a shelter, finding comfort by telling each other how we got there. We may be at a twelve-step meeting where each of us begins the road to healing by standing to say, "I have a problem, and here is my story." It's in sharing our stories that we come to see each other in light of the human joys and struggles that bind us both now and then.

Law is meant to separate the good from the bad; facts are meant to separate the knowledgeable from the ignorant. But stories are meant to bring us toward each other in a sharing of common ground to solve a common problem to reach a common goal. We test the fruit of that common ground by asking whether it serves to promote the biblical vision of justice and blessing for all nations and peoples.

Yes, the Bible tells us that before this ultimate vision can be achieved, there will be judgment to separate the wheat from the chaff. And the parable Jesus tells about that judgment gives us specific instruction. We mortals are to leave the field alone, allowing the weeds and the wheat to grow together, until such time as the one capable of true justice comes to sort things out. Judgment about who is or is not fit to enter the Holy City or enjoy that peaceful, holy mountain is God's job, not ours.

Our job in the here and now is simply to share the stories of God's people—their struggles and triumphs, their sins and their virtues—and through that sharing to build a community that can support each other on the road. As it happens, God gave us a tool for doing just that. It's a book of stories called the Bible, stories that mirror both the best and the worst of ourselves, bound into a framework of hope that the paradise once lost can be, in the end, regained.

Acknowledgments

Books are not easy to write, and I am grateful to many who helped me carve out time, space, and the peace of mind to make this one possible. Worthy of special note are Alastair and Chris Saunders, who opened their summer home to me for a month in the dead of winter so that I could gather my thoughts and write in Nova Scotia at the water's edge. And, as if that were not enough, Alastair continued to offer his intellectual prowess as a reader for my drafts and a sounding board for my wandering mind long after I had returned home. Without both of those gifts, this book would never have seen the light of day.

There's also a good chance that this book is seeing the light of *your* day because Bishop Will Willimon agreed to provide the foreword. Gratitude seems like too small a word to express how that act of grace by a man of his stature made me feel.

Acknowledgments

I am also grateful to the BTS Center in Portland, Maine. Their grant allowed me to run "The Great Bible Experiment: Exploring the Bible in America's Least Bible-Minded Cities" in September 2016. Engaging those four events in cities across the Northeast helped shape and inform the ideas in this book.

I am also grateful to my editor, Lil Copan, for her patience and persistence in seeing this through to completion, for her insight, and for her guidance in honing and shaping my words. She has made this a far better book, as has Senior Editor Mary Hietbrink. And I extend my gratitude to others at Eerdmans who work behind the scenes and who agreed to take a chance on my work. It is an honor to be published by a company that has published so many scholars I admire.

Questions for Personal Reflection and Group Discussion

Chapter 1

1. What is one story from your family of origin that you enjoy telling? Do you feel that story defines your family in some way? If so, how?
2. Do you know any stories about your ancestors? Do those stories help you understand your family now?
3. What was your favorite fictional story as a child? Looking back on it now, did it form who you are in any way? If you could have the life of one fictional character, who would it be and why?
4. If you're scrolling through categories of movies or looking over the topics in a bookstore, where do you head first? Explain.
5. Have you ever felt like there was a story you couldn't

tell to certain people? If so, why? Are there stories
you've never told anyone?

6. Has another person's story ever made you uncomfortable? If so, how did you respond?

7. Do you have a favorite Bible story? Do you have a Bible story you would cut out of the Bible if you could?
What is it about those stories that either delights or
troubles you?

8. Have you ever had a relationship suffer because one
person wouldn't listen to the stories of the other?

Chapter 2

1. What sources do you turn to if you want to find out if
something is factual?

2. If someone were painting a portrait of your mother,
what would it have to show for you to call it a "true"
portrait of her?

3. What fictional story do you find to be absolutely true to
life?

4. If God offered you a relationship on the condition that
you tried to live by the Ten Commandments, would
you accept? Why or why not?

5. If you could change one thing about the public dis-

cussion surrounding the Ten Commandments, what would it be and why?

6. If you had to sum up the truth conveyed by the story of Jonah, what would it be?

7. Do you believe there is absolute truth, or is truth all relative to individuals in their own time and place? What do you make of Paul's claim that we see only "through a glass, darkly"?

8. Using more than just "yes" or "no," how would you answer the question "Is the Bible true?"

Chapter 3

1. What are your own views on the inspiration of Scripture? Do they differ from those of your faith community? Is accepting a certain view a requirement in your faith tradition?

2. Do you find questions about the inspiration of the Bible to be interesting? Unsettling? Important? Beside the point? Have you ever thought about the question of the Bible's inspiration before?

3. Are you starting to see a difference in viewing the Bible as story? Does the story lens make sense to you? What questions does it bring up?

4. What does being "fully human and fully God" mean to

you—either when spoken about Jesus or about the Bible? How would you describe the relationship of God to the Bible?

5. If you believe in God, how do you see God at work in day-to-day life?

6. Who are people—famous or ordinary, living or past—who you believe did or are doing God's work in the world?

Chapter 4

1. What is the very first Bible story you remember hearing? Who were the chain of storytellers that brought the story to you? How did you respond to the story?

2. Have you ever heard someone use their authority to preach or teach about the Bible in a way you thought manipulated the text to their own advantage? How did you respond?

3. Who are the people—past or present, in any field—who you believe used or use their power wisely? Do you see restraint as an example of power or weakness?

4. Has a biblical reference or sign of influence ever popped up in a place you never expected it?

5. In what ways do you see the view of the Bible being shaped in the public sphere today? Is that influence

positive or negative in your view? If negative, how can it be countered with something more positive?

6. What role, if any, do you think the Bible should play in government and public institutions?

7. What do you think the Bible means in giving human beings "dominion" over the earth?

Chapter 5

1. Think of a time you were really afraid. How did you get through it? Did someone or something offer you hope? Did getting through it make the next time any easier?

2. Were you familiar with the story about the snake on a pole in Numbers 21 before reading this chapter? Does looking at that passage in the context of the larger biblical story make a difference to you?

3. Have you ever heard a Bible story that made you afraid? What was it? How did you respond?

4. Have you ever heard a Bible story that gave you hope? What was it? Did you ever share it with others?

5. Do you feel like your life is moving from fear toward hope or the other way round? Or are you stuck?

6. What do you believe about Hell? Where did that belief come from?

7. 1 John 4:18 says that perfect love drives out fear. Does that ring true for you?

8. Do you see the Bible as a hopeful book? Why or why not?

Chapter 6

1. If someone asked you "Why do bad things happen to good people?," what would you say?

2. Do you seek out stories of suffering, either in books, movies, plays, or other media? Why or why not?

3. If a story describes a type of suffering or loss that you have experienced yourself, do you find it helps or hurts your healing process?

4. Have you ever had friends like Job's friends who insist you're responsible for your suffering when you're not? Have you ever been one of Job's friends to someone else?

5. Many people assume that those stuck in poverty brought it on themselves and that helping them is enabling bad behavior. How would the writer of Job respond to this view? How about the parable of the Good Samaritan?

6. It is difficult and draining to care for those who suffer. Have you experienced this? How did you renew yourself?

7. Have you ever been a "good Samaritan" to someone? Have you ever been one of the people who walked on by and didn't help for whatever reason? Have you ever been the guy wounded in the road? Did anyone help? Does that parable connect with the story of your life in any way?

Chapter 7

1. Have you ever witnessed something you felt was a miracle? How did you respond?

2. How do you typically respond to the miracles recounted in the Bible? Do you think they happened? Do you think they're superstitions of a less enlightened age? Or something in-between? Do you believe there are angels? Demons?

3. Does calling miracles "signs" change anything for you? If so, in what way?

4. Do you like surprises or other unexpected events, or do you prefer to know exactly what's in front of you all the time? How would you gauge your own personal tolerance for mystery and unexpected events?

5. What do you believe about the events of Jesus's death and resurrection? Did they literally happen? Are they

metaphors? How much do the answers to those questions matter to you?

6. Is examining the Bible as story making a difference for you? Are you feeling dizzy? Are some things less problematic for you than they were before? Is the story lens problematic for you in some way? Why?

7. What role do you think humility plays (or should play) in reading the Bible?

8. How comfortable are you living with an unanswered question? Does this depend on the kind of question?

Chapter 8

1. What role do you think imagination plays in religion? Do you find that helpful? Why or why not?

2. When have you worked with another person or group of people toward a common goal? Do you prefer working with a group or by yourself? Do you see the Bible as encouraging one or the other?

3. We live in a very polarized time. What kind of vision do you think could unite us? Do you think the Bible offers such a vision, or do you see the Bible as part of the problem?

4. Are there any toxic stories that once informed your life

that you have since rejected? If so, did you find different stories to replace them?

5. What do you see as toxic stories in our culture? How can we shift the narrative?

6. What source(s) do you trust for information? Why do you trust them? Is the Bible on that list?

7. What does living a biblical life mean to you?

8. Has this book changed anything about the way you view the Bible?